Who Cares?

God's Path for the Caregiver

Valeri Miller

Cover and text design by Diane King, dkingdesigner.com

Scripture taken from the King James Version. Public domain.

Library of Congress Control Number: 2013903082

ISBN 978-0-9890239-1-7

Printed in the United States of America.

Dedication

This book is dedicated to all the wonderful caregivers who willingly give of their time to care for their loved ones.

Special thanks to my husband for his unwavering support.

To my children, Joshua and Jennifer: your day will come, so be prepared!

Special thanks to Janet Shay. Without her planting, watering, and nurturing the idea of this book, I would never have attempted the project.

> "If any of you lack wisdom, let him ask of God, that giveth to all men liberally, and upbraideth not; and it shall be given him" (James 1:5).

Contents

Introduction 7
1 Who Loves Old People? 11
2 Trust 15
3 Faithfulness 31
4 Forgive Whom? 43
5 Boundaries 59
6 Caregiver Burnout 71
7 Independence Versus Dependence 79
8 End-of-Life Care 87
9 Caregiving Is Over—Now What? 95
10 For Pastors and Church Families 107
APPENDIX A A-Z Scriptures for Meditation/Memorization 115
APPENDIX B Medical Terminology 119
APPENDIX C List of Important Documents 123
APPENDIX D Favorite Caregiver Tips. 127
APPENDIX E Additional Resources 131
BIBLIOGRAPHY 133

Introduction

I met my husband, a family practice doctor finishing his residency, while I was a Registered Nurse working at the same hospital. Our wedding took place at our church, and to accommodate our co-workers, we held the reception in the hospital dining room.

We settled in a rural community where everyone knew our names. Whether it was a relative or friend or one of my husband's patients, we seldom went out to eat that we did not meet someone who stopped at our table to talk. We lived in a lovely split-level home. It held a special appeal for me because it was surrounded by woods on three sides, full of beautiful singing birds year round.

Three years after we were married, God blessed us with a red-headed son. My red-headed father was thrilled. When our son was two years old, I began teaching his Sunday school class of two- and three-year-olds (twenty-five years later I am still teaching the same age group of precious little children). Three years after our son was born, we were again blessed—this time with a blond, brown-eyed daughter.

After we had been living in our home for about seven years, my in-laws moved into the house across the street. The first thing my father-in-law did was to trim back all of the lower tree branches so he could have a better view of our house. I was not sure how I would adapt to in-laws living so close, but I saw very quickly what a treasure it was for our children to have their grandparents living right across the street. A few years later, my own parents and grandmother moved within a mile of us.

Content and busy taking care of my husband and our children, I enjoyed weekly visits with my parents and grandmother when I could fit them into my schedule. My in-laws took pleasure in babysitting for their grandchildren, and every Sunday after church, we ate dinner at their home. On Monday nights we went over for leftovers. Wednesday night was pizza night, and they often took us out to eat on Friday or Saturday. Cooking became a rare occasion, and I did not mind at all! By 1995, we were living the American dream. My "perfect little world" was complete and I was delighted.

God, in His wisdom, knew I had some things to learn. In March 1995 a series of trials began that I certainly would never have chosen on my own. As time has passed, I can honestly say that I am thankful for the journey I traveled because of those trials.

Are you a caregiver for a parent or grandparent? Do your caregiving responsibilities sometimes stretch you so thin that you feel as if you are going to snap? Have you ever asked yourself if anyone cares or understands what you are going through?

These feelings are not uncommon. I asked those very same questions many times throughout my seventeen-year role as a caregiver.

A parent's responsibility is to care for their children until they are old enough and mature enough to be on their own. In that regard, those who are blessed to have children already understand a little about the responsibilities of a caregiver. At some point in our lives the child/parent roles reverse. We may be called upon to become a caregiver for a parent, a grandparent, or an extended family member. As I see it, during every phase of life, we are either being cared for by someone, or we are caring for someone.

Going back to the subject of children for a moment, a mother of a young child sometimes feels at the end of her rope. Is her child ever going to be potty trained? How can she help her son with his math when she got a "D" in algebra herself? Just as parental challenges eventually pass, so do the responsibilities of caring for an aging loved one. No matter how difficult our task may be at the time, one day we will look back and realize it was only a blip on the road of life.

I wrote this book after seventeen years of caring for more than one aging family member. I realized that many of my struggles were struggles others also face daily. I came to understand that God cares and wants to conform us to His image. God wants to use us in the lives of those for whom we are caregiving. My heart's desire is that the truths I am sharing will encourage and bless other caregivers.

"Who cares?" we may ask. We can be assured that God cares, and He will be there with us through every step of our caregiving journey.

-1-

Who Loves Old People?

The following poem has been credited to numerous authors and published in many different versions. This is my version:

What Do You See?

What do you see when you're looking at me?
A crabby old man, not very wise,
Uncertain of habit, with faraway eyes,
Who dribbles his food and makes no reply
When you say in a loud voice "I do wish you'd try"
Who resisting or not lets you do as you will,
With bathing and feeding, the long day to fill?
Is that what you're thinking? Is that what you see?

I'll tell you who I am as I sit here so still,
As I do your bidding, as I eat at your will.
I am a small child of ten with father and mother,
Brothers and sisters who love one another.
A young boy of sixteen with wings on his feet
Dreaming very soon a sweet girl he will meet.
A groom at twenty my heart gives a leap
Remembering the vows I promised to keep.

I'm twenty-five now and have a child of my own.
I've turned forty and my young sons are grown.

I'm past fifty and once again babies play around my knee.
Nearing seventy, dark days are upon me.
My wife is now dead.
I look to the future and shudder with dread.

I'm now an old man and nature is cruel.
The body, it crumbles; grace and vigor depart,
But inside this old carcass, a young man still dwells,
And now and again my battered heart swells.
I remember the joys, I remember the pain.
I am loving and living life over again.
I ask you again, what do you see?
Please open your eyes, open and see
Not a crabby old man,
Look closer and see me!

The caregiver's journey takes place in a world full of conflict in both emotions and expectations. It is a world a caregiver often wishes to escape—yet never wants to leave.

As a caregiver, have you ever experienced exhaustion, frustration, anger, fear, or resentment? On the other hand, have you had days when you encountered contentment, joy, laughter, and just plain fun?

On any given day of the week, or any hour of the same day, a caregiver can ride the emotional rollercoaster of either set of feelings. It is not what set of emotions we experience, but how much we dwell on them. From a Christian perspective, how are we to handle these emotions? Life as a caregiver can sometimes be difficult. We really need God's help and God's Spirit in our lives to enable us to respond appropriately and compassionately. As we study and discuss the scope of caregiving, we will focus on several specific issues.

Chapter two discusses the concept of trust, and what better place to start than at the very beginning of the Bible with Eve in the Garden of Eden?

In chapter three, we look at faithfulness. We will go to the book of 2 Samuel and study the life of Rizpah. I will challenge us to go to our Bibles and search out what Rizpah has to say about faithfulness. Her story is an amazing lesson to all of us.

The fourth chapter deals with forgiveness. How do we forgive, and on whom are we asked to bestow forgiveness? What if we have been abused by a parent and are now being called upon to act as their caregiver? How can we personally overcome resentment, anger, or bitterness, let alone see to this parent's daily needs?

Chapter five takes us to the subject of boundaries. Yes, we do need to set boundaries when caring for a loved one, especially in our own home. How much of our personal space should we be expected to give up to meet their needs?

Caregiver burnout is covered in chapter six. There were times when I wished one or another of my loved ones would go ahead and die. What should we do when these thoughts enter our minds?

Next, we will focus on the recipient. Do we treat our elderly parents or grandparents with the respect they deserve? Their loss of independence can be very humiliating. How can we help them manage, and even welcome, the inevitable change from independence to dependence?

Chapter eight brings us to end-of-life care. What are the doctors really saying? How do we say "goodbye"?

In chapter nine, we look at grief and what happens when caregiving is over. How do we get our lives back to normal, and exactly what is the new normal?

Finally, we address opportunities and responsibilities for pastors and church families. How can they assist with the spiritual and physical support of a caregiver? What special needs do surviving caregivers have once their loved one has died?

Each chapter always begins with *The purpose of caregiving: Showing love to everyone else, while giving GOD the work of changing MY heart.*

God taught me many, many things I needed to learn and work on when I took my own caregiving journey. I went down that road kicking and screaming more times than I care to admit, but God didn't give up on me. I have learned so much. I pray this book will bring hope and encouragement as we gain a new perspective on our roles as caregivers.

-2-

Trust

> Now the serpent was more subtle than any beast of the field which the LORD God had made. And he said unto the woman, Yea, hath God said, ye shall not eat of every tree of the garden? And the woman said unto the serpent, we may eat of the fruit of the trees of the garden: But of the fruit of the tree which is in the midst of the garden, God hath said, ye shall not eat of it, neither shall ye touch it, lest ye die. And the serpent said unto the woman, Ye shall not surely die: For God doth know that in the day ye eat thereof, then your eyes shall be opened and ye shall be as gods knowing good and evil and when the woman saw that the tree was good for food, and that it was pleasant to the eyes, and a tree to be desired to make one wise, She took of the fruit thereof and did eat, and gave also unto her husband with her; and he did eat (Genesis 3:1-6).

The Scriptures show us Eve's downfall as we see her actions described in this passage: the lust of the flesh, the lust of the eyes, and the pride of life. She heard, she saw, and she took. But what was Eve's temptation really all about? I believe the root of Eve's temptation is best described with the following questions: Would she love God and God alone? Would she trust God and God alone? Would she unconditionally obey God and God alone?

We can apply these same questions to caregiving as we try to understand what caregiving is really all about. Will we love God and God alone? Will we trust God and God alone? Will we unconditionally obey God and God alone?

Caregiving demands much from us. It demands our time, our property, and our love. In reality, it demands our total being. According to C. P. Hia in *Our Daily Bread*, "As a result of adult children neglecting their responsibilities, some elderly parents in Singapore are forced to seek financial and physical help from charities and other state agencies. Speaking about this escalating situation, a government official said we cannot legislate love."[1] But in Scripture, this is exactly what God does—He legislates love.

> Jesus said unto him thou shall love the Lord thy God with all thy heart and with all thy soul and with all thy mind. This is the first and great commandment and the second is like unto it, Thou shall love thy neighbor as thyself (Matthew 22:37-39).

So we are commanded to love and to love some more. We are to love our God, and we are to love our neighbor. This is a double love command. We think of our neighbor as someone who lives next door or down the street, but what about the person for whom we are caregiving? Our loved ones are also our neighbors whether they are living in our home, in an assisted living facility, or in a nursing home down the street. They are someone God has commanded us to love. We know and understand we are commanded to love God. Is it as easy to comprehend that we are commanded to love our neighbor or a family member?

When does God expect us to love others? Does God expect us to love them when they complain or say unkind things about us? We can easily give love when we have no opposition and everything is going our way. But showing love to someone who consistently complains and can never be satisfied requires an extra measure of God's grace. This is not an easy command to follow.

Does God expect us to love others when they are demanding and want what they want now? I am very selfish. I do not like to have someone tell me what to do. I definitely do not want to be told when to do it or how to do it. While I prefer not having anyone else make demands on my time, is this a proper response to God's command to love?

Sometimes even working up the desire to demonstrate love in a world of chaos is beyond our human capabilities apart from God's power and grace. We have weathered 9/11, earthquakes, tsunamis, hurricanes, and wars. The world does not make sense. My world certainly did not make sense when my mother passed away while my little girl was in kindergarten. My five-year-old daughter could not understand why I had no explanation for God allowing such a tragedy. My mother had taught my daughter's kindergarten class at a local Christian school. One Friday, Mother did not feel well and went home from school early. By Monday afternoon, she was in so much pain that my husband, a physician, admitted her to the hospital for pain control and tests to determine what was wrong.

On Tuesday morning, while I was helping Mother to the bedside commode, she remarked, "Well, I sure have come a long way—still using a slop bucket!" Those were the last coherent words my mother said to me. Within several hours, she had suffered a massive stroke. She died four days later.

My daughter, Jenni, cried every day the entire next year because Grandma was not her teacher anymore. Jenni's first grade teacher, Mrs. D., was tremendous. More than once she stayed to teach even when she was not feeling well. Mrs. D. knew Jenni was terrified that if her teacher went home sick, she would die just like her grandma had died. Mrs. D was a great example to me of modeling love for others—no matter what the age. At that point, she was a caregiver for my first grader!

Overnight, because of the death of my mother, I inherited the role of caregiver for my grandmother and my father. This new responsibility continued for the next seventeen years and eventually expanded to include caring for my in-laws, and nursing them through several health scares and surgeries. At one point, I was caring for my mother-in-law upstairs in my home and my father downstairs at the same time.

We are expected to demonstrate God's love even when we are hurting at the same time a loved one is suffering. Out of love, we make every effort to protect them and keep them comfortable both physically and emotionally. There are times we may feel a need to hide our own emotional or physical pain so as not to increase our loved one's suffering. When Jenni was hurting because of the loss of her grandma, I was strong for her on the drive to school, but I cried all the way home. Like my daughter, I experienced the emotional pain of separation from my mother. I was suffering, too, but I knew it was best for Jenni to protect her by showing sacrificial love—concealing my own deep sorrow so she did not have to witness it.

My daughter was expected to love the teacher who took over for her grandmother for the remainder of the school year. This sort of love is not easy. The focus of this chapter is on trust. "Trust in the Lord with all thine heart, and lean not unto thine own understanding. In all thy ways acknowledge him and he shall direct thy paths" (Proverbs 3:5-6). We do not need to understand the whys of life, but we do need to trust God in every circumstance. Finally, it comes down to knowing and believing who God is and trusting the promise of His grace to enable us to glorify Him through our weaknesses:

> And he said unto me, My grace is sufficient for thee: for My strength is made perfect in weakness. Most gladly therefore will I rather glory in my infirmities, that the power of Christ may rest upon me (2 Corinthians 12:9).

We may not always sense His presence, but God's Holy Spirit enables us to love and believe that nothing can separate us from His love:

> For I am persuaded, that neither death, nor life, nor angels, nor principalities, nor powers, nor things present, nor things to come, nor height, nor depth, nor any other creature, shall be able to separate us from the love of God, which is in Christ Jesus our Lord (Romans 8:38-39).

Most of us acknowledge that we are expected to show love when we recognize someone's visible needs, but what about their invisible needs? For me, it is easy to love and care for those who are in pain due to an obvious physical need. I had wanted to be a nurse since I was ten years old. I believe God gave me the heart of compassion necessary for that profession. If I see someone in pain, I am there to help in a heartbeat. Yet, I had trouble looking past the outward appearance and bravado of those for whom I was giving long-term care. I did not grasp the underlying loneliness and emotional trauma they experienced. I did not see the invisible feelings of abandonment nor identify the signs of depression. I had to learn to be sensitive to the invisible needs as well as the visible.

How can we recognize the invisible needs of those for whom we are caregiving? I was unaware of the invisible loneliness my mother-in-law felt after her husband died. She would telephone me five to six times a day to chat. "What are you doing? What are your plans for today?" she would ask. I considered these questions nosy. I felt this information was none of her business and evaded answering whenever possible. Now, I understand she was not prying. She was crying out for love and compassion. She desperately needed to be a part of someone else's world. Today, I ask those same types of questions to my married daughter. We need to be careful how we demonstrate compassion and love to our parents, because our children are watching! If we take a moment right now and think about our loved one, what invisible needs would we see that we have previously overlooked?

We are expected to love when things are not going as planned. I certainly had not planned to be thrust into the role of caregiving at the age of thirty-eight. I had two children, ages five and eight. Taking them to school each day meant a thirty-minute drive one way. It seemed there were not enough hours to get everything done between morning drop-off and afternoon pick-up. With the addition of two elderly people to care for, I had to spread myself thinner!

How many different directions are we being asked to go at the same time? How do we respond when one more responsibility is added to our already full agendas? While God designed us with an ability to do multiple tasks, we must be careful to show love and patience while fulfilling those tasks. Are we caring for our loved ones out of a sense of duty or a sense of love?

I am often impatient. My father could always tell when I was not focused on the task at hand and would sense my desire to get the job done quickly rather than serving him out of a heart of love and patience. Our hearts must daily refocus on God's grace and empowering Holy Spirit to enable us to love when we are too busy to stop and think. God has promised He will not give us more than we are able to handle but will give us the ability and strength to accomplish everything He has put on our plates. Our responsibility is to keep an attitude of love and compassion even when our schedules are overbooked.

At the moment we are giving care, we should strive to make our loved ones feel that they are the most important people in the world. It is difficult to be patient and loving when we want to hurry and get to the next item on our agenda. While we may not realize it, our impatience shows, and it can be hurtful to someone who is already feeling that they are in the way. Isaiah 40:31 has always been one of my favorite verses of encouragement during my busiest days:

> But they that wait upon the Lord shall renew their strength; they shall mount up with wings as eagles; they shall run, and not be weary; and they shall walk, and not faint.

We are also expected to love when others do not meet our expectations. I am very particular. I like things done my way, in my time, and how I say for it to be done. My mother used to say, "If I say jump, you do not ask how high, you just start jumping!" I had to learn there are other ways to accomplish the same goal, and if it does not get done by a certain time, it is okay. The world will not stop if everything we had planned does not get done as we had hoped it would on any given day. The laundry and house cleaning will wait. Even the dishes will wait for at least a day, if it means we showed patience and allowed a loved one to get things done at their speed. Not only should we show patience, but we should also treasure each and every moment with them. After the months or years of caregiving are over, we will realize how fast the time went; we will cherish and remember those long, yet special, moments.

We are expected to love others when they are irritable, obstinate, or unreasonable. We need to love that person with dementia, even when they have no clue what they are doing. This kind of love requires a higher level of patience than we ever thought we were capable of demonstrating. We need to answer their questions each time they ask, whether it is once or ten times a day. We also need to answer in the correct tone of voice and with the right attitude. It is not helpful or necessary to remind them it is the tenth time they have asked that question in the last hour.

I know firsthand how difficult it is to be patient and continue to answer respectfully! It is painful to see our once strong, vibrant parent now reduced to incoherent babbling. We may experience overwhelming emotional pain when a parent no longer remembers who we are or why we are in their room. Accomplishing only one task each day can take more prayer and ingenuity than we knew we were capable of apart from God's grace. Most people would not be satisfied with the accomplishment of only one task on any given day. That outlook changes when we become caregivers. I would never have thought such a simple pleasure as getting a loved one dressed in the morning without a fight would bring such a feeling of accomplishment.

We have been talking about the times we are expected to love others, but what motivates us to be a caregiver? Do we give care because it is expected, or are we caught up in our own daily lives and too busy to think about another's needs?

My husband was an only child, so all of the caregiving responsibilities fell to me. There was no one else available to give his parents the extra care and attention they needed every day, and I did not work outside of the home. That made me the logical caregiver. I would have preferred my in-laws move to an assisted living facility, where they could have had daily stimulation through activities and conversation with other people. They were a very loving, patient couple who never met a stranger, and were always praying for people they met on their daily trips around town. I am not as much of a people person. I used to be annoyed when they knew everyone's name in every store around town. I do well to remember my own name some days. I had my life and my kids and not much time for their life, even though they lived right across the street.

Through caregiving, God taught me how selfish I had become. I slowly awoke to the realization that this trait did not please God. It was a characteristic I drastically needed to address in my life and am still working to change. I am trying to remember people's names and at the very least, their faces. I am making a great effort to greet them with a word of encouragement just as my in-laws showed me by their example.

What is our compassion meter showing today? Notice, I said today, as the apostle Paul said in Philippians 3:12-14:

> Not as though I had already attained, either were already perfect: but I follow after, if that I may apprehend that for which also I am apprehended of Christ Jesus. Brethren, I count not myself to have apprehended: but this one thing I do, forgetting those things which are behind, and reaching forth unto those things which are before, I press toward the mark for the prize of the high calling of God in Christ Jesus.

Maybe our motive in giving care is one born out of necessity. Perhaps there is no one else who is willing to or can assume the responsibility. This particular motive can become a source of family conflict if not guarded carefully. If there are other siblings, it is easy to become bitter when they cannot, or will not, help with the caregiving responsibilities. Sometimes I would call my siblings and ask them to stay with my father so my husband and I could go out of town. Usually, they were very accommodating, but occasionally they were unable to help. Unfortunately, I did not always respond properly. Sometimes I got mad and cried, and other times I became angry or jealous. These reactions are the very negative attributes God warns us to avoid. He dealt with me more than once about my reactions when circumstances did not go my way. Thankfully, my siblings and I have a good relationship, but sin can easily enter the door of any caregiving situation, if we are not continually protecting that relationship.

Do we give care out of a sense of pride or self-importance, thinking we are the only one who can do it best? This is a dangerous attitude. Yes, maybe we can do it best. I was a nurse and my husband was a family practice physician. We felt we could take care of our parents best because we were both intellectually and practically prepared. But is that all that is required? Absolutely not! If our loved ones are in their right minds and able to make their own decisions, it is important to allow them to decide where they want to live.

Then we must respect their decisions. Sometimes, it can be hurtful if they choose to live with another sibling.

I do not know the reason, maybe it was a father/daughter bond, but my dad wanted to live with me. Dad's choice filled me with a sense of pride. I did not find out until much later that my brother would have loved to have been my dad's primary caregiver, especially when Dad was physically able to walk and help around the house with small tasks. Dad loved to tell stories from the "good old days" and occasionally broke out in song at the dinner table. My brother wanted his children to experience some of those special memories of their grandfather. Dad chose to live with me, but I should have been more sensitive to my brother's desires. Keeping the lines of communication open with all of the family, both the parents and the children, is vital to a healthy, God-honoring family relationship.

We also need to be prepared if our loved one makes the choice to stay exactly where they have always lived and refuses to move. We can become very frustrated, angry, or overbearing when trying to get our loved one to move where we want them to move, and they refuse to follow our wishes. We need to recognize their decision as either a means of control, a fear of change, a need for a sense of stability, or all of the above. Change at any age is frightening, and we must respect that fear. Yet, the manner in which we present the need for change can make a huge difference.

First, we can present our appeal in the form of a question such as: "Do you think it is best for you to continue living alone, or would you like to move somewhere else, either in with another family member or to an assisted living home?" Making our loved ones feel as though they are in control and making these life changing decisions will benefit everyone involved.

Another way to present change is to offer it as a personal favor for us. My parents lived five hours away. I suggested how helpful it would be, as they got older and had more medical needs, if they would move closer to our home. They made the decision to move one mile away from where we lived, and I will always be grateful for their decision.

My in-laws also lived out of town and decided they would move into the house across the street from us at their retirement. My mother-in-law, Margaret, had never lived anywhere else. When she married, she spent her first year of marriage living with her mother-in-law. During that first year, Margaret's father died suddenly and my in-laws moved back into her family home. I will forever have tremendous respect for their willingness to give up the family home and land, in order to move two hours away from everything and everyone they had ever known. Over the years, I slowly realized having the grandparents so near was a huge blessing for the grandchildren. We need to be prepared to allow them to move near us. Remember, God knows exactly where they need to be located in relation to us, and He will change our hearts as necessary to deal with the close or far location of our loved ones.

The "I can do it best" syndrome can manifest itself in the home, too. My father did anything I asked and ate everything I fed him. If my husband took Dad's meal to him, Dad would say he was not hungry, and he would refuse to eat! My husband learned to say, "Valeri wants you to eat this," or "Valeri asked me to bring this to you." As long as my dad thought the meal was from me, he would eat it. This scenario can be a source of irritation for other family members. Be careful not to foster a prideful "I can do it best" attitude. My husband was very understanding and patient and it became amusing to hear how many different ways he could say, "Valeri said."

Through every phase of caregiving, we need encouragement. In order to fulfill our responsibilities, be encouraged in our walk with the Lord, and maintain a testimony within our family, we need to be in the Scriptures daily. Matthew 4:4 encourages us in this regard. "But He answered and said, It is written, Man shall not live by bread alone, but by every word that proceedeth out of the mouth of God." Joshua 1:8 is even more specific:

> This book of the law shall not depart out of thy mouth; but thou shalt meditate therein day and

> night, that thou mayest observe to do according to all that is written therein: for then thou shalt make thy way prosperous, and then thou shalt have good success.

While I realize this was speaking specifically to Joshua before he entered the Promised Land, it is valid for us today on our caregiving journey. Only by reading and meditating on the Scriptures can we begin to understand what promises and hope there are for us day by day and minute by minute. APPENDIX A has a list of Scriptures for memorization or meditation from A-Z. So many of these verses are applicable to the caregiver!

Not only do we need to be in the Scriptures daily, but according to 1 Thessalonians 5:17, we also need to "pray without ceasing," as we carry out various tasks for our loved ones. Psalm 52:8b is a good Scripture to meditate on: "I trust in the mercy of God for ever and ever." God is faithful and ready to show mercy even when we mess up. Many times I had to ask the Lord to "keep the door of my lips" (Psalm 141:3b).

Uplifting music is another source of encouragement. For a long time I kept the television blaring all day to keep me company. Eventually, I found I got so much more done and was in a better frame of mind, if I listened to music instead of the TV. I was less frustrated and annoyed when my dad called or rang his bell indicating he needed my help. Why not listen to uplifting music and meditate on what we have read in His word today? We will have a better attitude as we meet the demands on our time.

One advantage to being home all of the time and listening to uplifting music is the opportunity to sing along using whatever voice God has given us! I cannot carry a tune in a bucket, but I could sing along in my home while I was caregiving. My dad was hard of hearing and my lack of singing ability did not bother him in the least! God knows my heart, and to Him it was a pure melody of worship. And what can be better than worshipping our God in song?

> Make a joyful noise unto the Lord, all ye lands. Serve the Lord with gladness: come before His presence with singing. Know ye that the Lord He is God: it is He that hath made us, and not we ourselves; we are His people, and the sheep of His pasture. Enter into His gates with thanksgiving, and into His courts with praise: be thankful unto Him, and bless His name. For the Lord is good; His mercy is everlasting; and His truth endureth to all generations (Psalm 100:1-5).

Wow! These verses say it all in a nutshell. These are great verses to meditate on while we are caregiving to all generations.

Here is another special source of encouragement: Thank the Lord for pleasant and unpleasant tasks. "In everything give thanks: for this is the will of God in Christ Jesus concerning you" (1 Thessalonians 5:18).

I have to share a story regarding how I learned to choose to thank the Lord for unpleasant tasks. My grandmother was ninety-four when she passed away. She had continued to live in my dad's house for five years after my mother died. I did not realize my mother had always cleaned Grandmother's dentures. Several weeks after Mother's funeral, my grandmother pulled her dentures out of her mouth, placed them in my open hand, and told me they needed to be cleaned. I immediately went to the bathroom and looked down at those dentures. The pink portion of the denture that covers the roof of the mouth was black! I knew at that moment I had to make a choice. I could either gag and throw up—which is what I wanted to do—or I could say, "Lord, I am going to clean these dentures for you, because there is no one else I would ever do this for." Immediately, I had a sense of peace that I could choose to do this unpleasant task for the Lord. It was almost pleasant as I focused not on the grossness of the job, but on the Lord, as I finished scrubbing Grandmother's dentures. I used the same attitude when I had to accomplish other unpleasant jobs—like soaking and trimming my father's thick toenails, or assisting with bathing or toileting needs.

Another source of encouragement comes with a word of caution: We need to love our spouse and our children more, and love them on purpose. When we moved my mother-in-law into our home upstairs, I already had my father living downstairs, my daughter was a senior in high school, and my son was planning a wedding. Juggling these various family roles and responsibilities became difficult. I found I had to deliberately love my spouse more and make time for him after I got everyone else situated for the night. My daughter struggled with this, too. She resented the time it took to take care of my mother-in-law. She once said, "Mom, this is supposed to be my time. It is my senior year in high school and Grandma is interfering!" Wow, what an opportunity to teach both compassion and balance. Remember, we are training the next generation to ultimately take care of us.

The last source of encouragement is to be used only as a last resort. We may need to call a friend to vent. If we have reached the end of our rope and fear we may harm our self or our loved one, we need to call someone immediately. Every month the news has a story of elder abuse or neglect. Our best source of encouragement is first the Lord and His Word, along with uplifting music. However, God also uses other people and Christian friends to encourage us.

> Let us hold fast the profession of our faith without wavering; (for He is faithful that promised;) And let us consider one another to provoke unto love and to good works (Hebrews 10:23-24).

We do need to choose our friends wisely. We cannot let our time with friends become a gossip session or a pity party in which we relay how bad our life is going at the moment. We can receive benefit by talking with a friend who can pray with us, laugh with us, and encourage us. "A friend loveth at all times" (Proverbs 17:17a).

Proverbs 17:27-28 gives a caution to our sharing time:

> He that hath knowledge spareth his words: And a man of understanding is of an excellent spirit. Even a fool, when he holdeth his peace, is counted wise: And he that shutteth his lips is esteemed a man of understanding.

We have talked about our motivation for caregiving and sources of encouragement in our caregiving journey, but what do we do about the loss of our personal time? How do we cope with the drastic curtailment of our once active lifestyle? When we bring someone needing special care into our home, our life is put on hold in a sense. When we are bound to the house because of our caregiving responsibilities, we may feel trapped. More than ever before we need to embrace this time: "Be still and know that I am God" (Psalm 46:10a).

What else can we do to enhance our spiritual life during this time of enforced isolation? For one thing, we now have time for Bible reading and prayer like never before. We can experience an amazing understanding of the passage in Romans 8:38-39:

> For I am persuaded, that neither death, nor life, nor angels, nor principalities, nor powers, nor things present, nor things to come, Nor height, nor depth, nor any other creature, shall be able to separate us from the love of God, which is in Christ Jesus our Lord.

Neither circumstances nor people can separate us from the love of God. We may not have the external stimulation of other people, but we can have time, free from distractions, to increase our relationship with God and our understanding of His Word. Rest on this promise.

Psalm 112:7 is another verse of encouragement that has meant a lot to me: "He shall not be afraid of evil tidings: his heart is fixed, trusting in the Lord." We should not allow the time alone to dwell on the "what ifs" of our caregiving journey. In her book, *Ambushed by Grace*, Shelly Beach makes the following statement:

> As caregivers, we daily face the tough questions, the harsh realities, the heart-rending uncertainties. It is only as we gaze into the eyes of our loving God, fall into His embrace, and give way to His next steps that we will gain strength for the journey.[2]

God in His grace and wisdom is giving us time to conform to His image. We have not been put on a shelf; we have much to do. Let us trust in the Lord for strength on our caregiving journey.

-3-

Faithfulness

What do people do when they encounter a stinky, smelly mess? If it comes from their own child's diaper, they change it quickly and discard the evidence. I knew a father who put on a gas mask every time he had to change his child's diaper. I do not recommend going to that extreme, but what should our attitude and facial expressions be when we are asked to deal with a stinky mess?

The story of Rizpah is probably the most exciting lesson I have studied. The biblical account of Rizpah is one of those golden nuggets we have to search deeply for in the Scriptures. When we find such a nugget, we can benefit greatly by meditating on the lesson it teaches.

While Rizpah does not usually make the list of most prominent women in the Old Testament, she certainly has a lot to teach us about faithfulness to a stinky, smelly mess. The Old Testament introduces us to Rizpah and to her contemporary, Michal:

> And Saul had a concubine, whose name was Rizpah, the daughter of Aiah. Now the sons of Saul were Jonathan, and Ishui, and Melchishua: and the names of his two daughters were these; the name of the firstborn Merab, and the name of the younger Michal (2 Samuel 3:7a and 1 Samuel 14:49).

We learn Rizpah had two sons and was a concubine of Saul. In contrast, Michal was the youngest daughter of King Saul. Michal had no children, but she raised her five nephews as her own. As we compare these two women, we are able to apply their behavior to our lives and learn a wonderful lesson. The following Scripture passage is lengthy, but I encourage us to read it completely in order to understand the background of the time and place in which Rizpah lived.

> Then there was a famine in the days of David three years, year after year; and David enquired of the Lord. And the Lord answered, It is for Saul, and for his bloody house, because he slew the Gibeonites. And the king called the Gibeonites, and said unto them; (now the Gibeonites were not of the children of Israel, but of the remnant of the Amorites; and the children of Israel had sworn unto them: and Saul sought to slay them in his zeal to the children of Israel and Judah.) Wherefore David said unto the Gibeonites, What shall I do for you? and wherewith shall I make the atonement, that ye may bless the inheritance of the Lord? And the Gibeonites said unto him, We will have no silver nor gold of Saul, nor of his house; neither for us shalt thou kill any man in Israel. And he said, What ye shall say, that will I do for you. And they answered the king, The man that consumed us, and that devised against us that we should be destroyed from remaining in any of the coasts of Israel, Let seven men of his sons be delivered unto us, and we will hang them up unto the Lord in Gibeah of Saul, whom the Lord did choose. And the king said, I will give them. But the king spared Mephibosheth, the son of Jonathan the son of Saul, because of the Lord's oath that was between them, between David and Jonathan the son of Saul.

> But the king took the two sons of Rizpah the daughter of Aiah, whom she bare unto Saul, Armoni and Mephibosheth; and the five sons of Michal the daughter of Saul, whom she brought up for Adriel the son of Barzillai the Meholathite: And he delivered them into the hands of the Gibeonites, and they hanged them in the hill before the Lord: and they fell all seven together, and were put to death in the days of harvest, in the first days, in the beginning of barley harvest.
>
> And Rizpah the daughter of Aiah took sackcloth, and spread it for her upon the rock, from the beginning of harvest until water dropped upon them out of heaven, and suffered neither the birds of the air to rest on them by day, nor the beasts of the field by night. And it was told David what Rizpah the daughter of Aiah, the concubine of Saul, had done. And David went and took the bones of Saul and the bones of Jonathan his son from the men of Jabeshgilead, which had stolen them from the street of Bethshan, where the Philistines had hanged them, when the Philistines had slain Saul in Gilboa: And he brought up from thence the bones of Saul and the bones of Jonathan his son; and they gathered the bones of them that were hanged. And the bones of Saul and Jonathan his son buried they in the country of Benjamin in Zelah, in the sepulchre of Kish his father: and they performed all that the king commanded. And after that God was intreated for the land (2 Samuel 21:1-14).

As we see, there was a famine in the land of Israel. King David questioned the Lord as to why this was happening. God told

David it was because of the sin of the former king, Saul, who slew the Gibeonites after they had been promised security. King David immediately went to the Gibeonites and asked how he could make things right and remove this curse from his land. The Gibeonites requested seven sons of Saul to be hung on a tree—sort of an eye-for-an-eye mentality. Today, we would be horrified by such a request, but King David gave Rizpah's two sons and Michal's five nephews to the Gibeonites to be executed by hanging. Let us back up and take a closer look at Michal:

> And David behaved himself wisely in all his ways; and the Lord was with him. Wherefore when Saul saw that he behaved himself very wisely, he was afraid of him. But all Israel and Judah loved David, because he went out and came in before them. And Saul said to David, Behold my elder daughter Merab, her will I give thee to wife: only be thou valiant for me, and fight the Lord's battles. For Saul said, Let not mine hand be upon him, but let the hand of the Philistines be upon him. And David said unto Saul, Who am I? and what is my life, or my father's family in Israel, that I should be son in law to the king? But it came to pass at the time when Merab Saul's daughter should have been given to David, that she was given unto Adriel the Meholathite to wife. And Michal Saul's daughter loved David: and they told Saul, and the thing pleased him. And Saul said, I will give him her, that she may be a snare to him, and that the hand of the Philistines may be against him. Wherefore Saul said to David, Thou shalt this day be my son in law in the one of the twain. And Saul commanded his servants, saying, Commune with David secretly, and say, Behold, the king hath delight in thee, and all his servants love thee: now therefore be the king's son in

> law. And Saul's servants spake those words in the ears of David. And David said, Seemeth it to you a light thing to be a king's son in law, seeing that I am a poor man, and lightly esteemed? And the servants of Saul told him, saying, On this manner spake David. And Saul said, Thus shall ye say to David, The king desireth not any dowry, but an hundred foreskins of the Philistines, to be avenged of the king's enemies. But Saul thought to make David fall by the hand of the Philistines. And when his servants told David these words, it pleased David well to be the king's son in law: and the days were not expired. Wherefore David arose and went, he and his men, and slew of the Philistines two hundred men; and David brought their foreskins, and they gave them in full tale to the king, that he might be the king's son in law. And Saul gave him Michal his daughter to wife. And Saul saw and knew that the Lord was with David, and that Michal Saul's daughter loved him (1 Samuel 18:14-28).

Michal was the daughter of King Saul, sister of Jonathan, and younger sister of Merab. Merab was promised to David for killing Goliath but was given instead to Adriel. When her father realized Michal was in love with David, he decided to use it to his advantage and hopefully get David killed by requiring him to kill the Philistines in order to become the king's son-in-law. However, much to Saul's disappointment, David accomplished the task, married Michal, and became the king's son-in-law. Nowhere does it say David loved Michal. Michal was used as a political pawn. Michal's marriage to David was the first of a chain of sad events in Michal's life. Let us read on in 1 Samuel regarding the next chapter in David and Michal's life:

> And Saul sought to smite David even to the wall with the javelin: but he slipped away out of Saul's

presence, and he smote the javelin into the wall: and David fled, and escaped that night. Saul also sent messengers unto David's house, to watch him, and to slay him in the morning: and Michal David's wife told him, saying, If thou save not thy life to night, to morrow thou shalt be slain. So Michal let David down through a window: and he went, and fled, and escaped. And Michal took an image, and laid it in the bed, and put a pillow of goats' hair for his bolster, and covered it with a cloth. And when Saul sent messengers to take David, she said, He is sick. And Saul sent the messengers again to see David, saying, Bring him up to me in the bed, that I may slay him. And when the messengers were come in, behold, there was an image in the bed, with a pillow of goats' hair for his bolster. And Saul said unto Michal, Why hast thou deceived me so, and sent away mine enemy, that he is escaped? And Michal answered Saul, He said unto me, Let me go; why should I kill thee? So David fled, and escaped, and came to Samuel to Ramah, and told him all that Saul had done to him. And he and Samuel went and dwelt in Naioth. (1 Samuel 19:10-18). But Saul had given Michal his daughter, David's wife, to Phalti the son of Laish, which was of Gallim. (1 Samuel 25:44).

Again, Saul tried to kill David, but Michal helped David escape, and she lied to her father for her husband. Her reward for this deceit was to be sent away to a new husband, Paltiel. David did not immediately go and rescue her. In fact, this forced marriage lasted for approximately twenty-two years. David had to have known how much Michal loved him and what she endured from her father after she helped David escape. David showed no appreciation for the fact that he owed his life to Michal. The Bible also gives no indication that David had any contact with Michal until after her father, King Saul, had died.

To solidify David's ascension to the throne, David finally demanded his wife back from Paltiel as a political move. According to 2 Samuel 3:13-16, Paltiel loved Michal:

> And he said, Well; I will make a league with thee: but one thing I require of thee, that is, Thou shalt not see my face, except thou first bring Michal Saul's daughter, when thou comest to see my face. And David sent messengers to Ishbosheth Saul's son, saying, Deliver me my wife Michal, which I espoused to me for an hundred foreskins of the Philistines. And Ishbosheth sent, and took her from her husband, even from Phaltiel the son of Laish. And her husband went with her along weeping behind her to Bahurim. Then said Abner unto him, Go, return. And he returned.

There is no indication that Paltiel and Michal had any children, nor does the Bible indicate she had any children with David. Later, David is said to have cursed her with barrenness for her disdain and dismay at his actions when bringing home the Ark of the Covenant (2 Samuel 6). At some point, her older sister, Merab, died. Michal adopted her five nephews and raised them as her own. In that day, not having children of her own was a source of great sorrow. Her nephews would have provided some comfort and enjoyment in her otherwise unsettled life.

We return to the Gibeonites in 2 Samuel 21:8, where they demand the lives of the seven sons of Saul, in order to avenge his murdering of so many of the Gibeonites. David delivered to them all five of the grandsons of Saul that Michal was raising as her own; he also delivered up the two sons of Rizpah. Michal is not mentioned again in Scripture. Probably the execution of her nephews broke her. Such a response is understandable, and with no further reference to her, I imagine she became depressed, withdrew from life, gave up, and disappeared.

While Michal was a princess, and as the first wife of David, the potential queen of Israel, Rizpah was only a concubine of King Saul. Webster's dictionary defines a concubine as, "a woman with whom a man cohabits without being married, and one having a recognized social status in a household below that of a wife." A concubine in biblical days had very few rights. She was primarily a child bearer. Rizpah had two sons by Saul. She also was a political pawn. According to 2 Samuel 3:7, after the death of Saul, Abner raped her in hopes it would validate his claim to the throne. This is all we know about Rizpah until the famine. With the famine, Rizpah teaches us a powerful lesson about faithfulness!

When Rizpah's two sons were taken by King David to be killed by being hung on a tree, unlike Michal, Rizpah did not disappear off the radar screen. Instead, 2 Samuel 21:10 tells us that for seven months (from the beginning of harvest, until water dropped upon them out of heaven) she sat at the foot of the tree where her sons were hanging. She chased away the birds of the air (circling vultures) and the beasts of the fields. She did not allow any creature to come near her sons' decaying bodies. We can be assured that those bodies rapidly began to smell, stink, and look disgusting! She did not give up even though no one else cared. She remained though no one else helped her. She chose to remain faithful no matter what!

We have no record in Scripture of Michal or anyone else helping Rizpah with this disgusting, smelly task. We do know she chose to stay at the job because of her love for her family members. Someone finally noticed and told King David of Rizpah's faithfulness. David told them to cut down the bodies and give them a proper burial. What a huge lesson for us. We can remain faithful when caring for our loved ones even during the thankless, disgusting, smelly tasks.

So what are some of the difficult or unpleasant tasks a caregiver is frequently asked to do? Do you mind dealing with wet beds, washing linens, giving showers, or bathing your loved one? Do you gag when you have to empty the bedside commode? Are you disgusted when you have to clean dirty dentures?

I am a nurse by training, but I am not immune to the smells and distaste of some of the more personal aspects of caregiving. I want to remain as faithful as Rizpah, but use sound practical tips for dealing with the stinky, smelly messes at the same time.

BATHING

My mother-in-law took a bath every day for most of her life. As it became harder and harder for her to get in and out of the tub, I had to learn how to help her with her bathing. We first tried the tub/shower bench in the tub, but she was too easily chilled because she was not able to sit down in the warm water. Next, I convinced her to try to shower by sitting on a small circular stool. She was amazed a shower felt so good and warm, and she felt clean afterwards. While she was taking a shower, I would put her clothes and towel in the clothes dryer for a few minutes to warm them. Elderly people are usually colder than others because of decreased circulation due to age or various medications. My mother-in-law, who weighed less than 100 pounds most of her life, really appreciated the warm towel and clothes. A note of caution: do not warm the towels or clothes in the microwave. I burned a hole in my dad's pajamas once—but only once!

My mother-in-law could not wash her hair by herself. After she had used the washcloth and cleaned as much as she could on her own, I would shampoo her hair before she got out of the shower. To help her feel beautiful, I used Velcro curlers to give her thin hair some curl. She had gone to the beauty shop every week for many years, so she really appreciated this small gesture.

TOILETING

Another unpleasant task is toileting. I kept a box of baby wipes and a wastebasket by the toilet so my dad could clean himself as needed. Eventually, I had to start cleaning him, so I added a box of latex gloves beside the box of wipes. We can do any unpleasant task with gloves!

My father eventually needed a bedside commode, so I learned to place a rubber mat (not a rug) under the commode to catch the drips. To keep the commode smelling fresh, I tried a wide variety of remedies including pine cleaner, bleach, and sprays. None of it worked. Most had odors that were too strong or lingered too long. My brother suggested an antiseptic mouthwash. I went to the dollar store and bought an inexpensive generic brand of either wintergreen or peppermint mouthwash. One capful—poured in the bedside commode after every emptying—killed germs, smelled great, and solved one stinky, smelly mess.

Both my mother-in-law and my father eventually had to use disposable underwear. Please, never ever call them diapers or adult diapers. Diapers are for babies, and we are showing disrespect to our elderly family members when we refer to them as wearing diapers. We need to be sensitive to our loved ones, and realize they may feel embarrassed having to resort to wearing protective underwear. I always referred to the disposable underwear either by its brand name or by calling it underwear. It took my dad longer to accept the need, because he was embarrassed to wear diapers. As we talked about the need for change, I asked him to consider wearing them for protection, and pointed out how much it would help me with the washing of clothes and linens. Once I presented the idea of it helping me, he was willing to switch from boxers to disposable underwear. It relieved him of leaky embarrassments and sure helped me with the daily laundry load.

NAIL CARE

Just the words "nail care" send feelings of dread through me. A number of elderly people have toenails that are thick and unattractive due to decreased circulation. This predisposes them to a fungal infection. While not contagious, it is unsightly. Trimming the toenails is one of those tasks for which I prayed every time: "Lord, this is for you because there is no one on earth for whom I would ever do it." I would inevitably be reminded of Christ's example to His disciples of humility, when he washed their feet. What a privilege to kneel before our loved one and care for their feet.

Start the nail care process by soaking their feet for about fifteen minutes in warm water before trimming the toenails. Soaking softens the nails and makes them much easier to trim. If you have ever had a pedicure, you know how wonderful it feels. My father had ticklish feet, but he did enjoy the warm foot soak and the nail trim.

Conventional clippers sometimes worked well enough to clip the smaller nails, but usually I used the plier-like nail cutters to clip the nails straight across—not curved and not too short. Due to poor circulation, nails often grow slower on older people, so do not trim them too short. Once the feet have been soaked and the nails trimmed, take this opportunity to smooth some lotion with aloe on their feet and legs.

ORAL CARE

Denture care can be one of the more unique challenges a caregiver faces. After that first episode of cleaning my grandmother's dentures, I never forgot to clean them regularly.

My father and my mother-in-law both had their original teeth, which presented a different challenge. After a light stroke, my father could not hold his toothbrush in his mouth for very long. I purchased a battery operated toothbrush for him, and that turned out to be the perfect solution. I had a spit dish and fresh water for him to rinse his mouth after he finished. Good oral hygiene is required at every age. With a little organization, we can get everything together, assist as much as necessary, and assure that the person for whom we are caregiving will feel much better after their mouth is clean. Remember, a decrease in appetite may be a sign of tooth pain or it may indicate a cavity.

Having revealed some of the unpleasant physical aspects of caregiving, I am reminded that we need to remember to accomplish all of these tasks in light of eternity. We can expect lots of hard work. We may feel unloved and used as a political pawn. Now and then, we may experience the desire to give up. But let us remember the example of Rizpah, rather than Michal, and remain faithful to our loved ones even during the disgusting, smelly tasks.

At age eighty-five, my father memorized Lamentations 3:21-23:

> This I recall to my mind, therefore have I hope. It is of the LORD's mercies that we are not consumed, because His compassions fail not. They are new every morning: great is thy faithfulness.

GOD is faithful. We can also be faithful.

-4-

Forgive Whom?

Forgiveness as defined by Webster's dictionary is the act of releasing from the guilt or penalty of an offense. Colossians 3:13 gives us one of many verses concerning forgiveness: "Forbearing one another, and forgiving one another, if any man have a quarrel against any: even as Christ forgave you, so also do ye."

We are daily faced with situations in which we must choose our response, in addition to how we will remember a given event long after it is over. I become annoyed when I have to wait at a doctor's office for an appointment more than ten minutes past the scheduled time. I know of an office where it is normal for patients to wait at least two to three hours to see the doctor. I have no patience with the front office staff that allows overbooking for that doctor, nor am I tolerant of the doctor who allows his patients to wait that long to see him. I know there are occasional emergencies, but not on a regular basis. So, how are we supposed to respond when a physician is late or unavailable? Ephesians 4:32 answers this question for us: "And be ye kind one to another, tenderhearted, forgiving one another, even as God for Christ's sake hath forgiven you."

Christ has forgiven me for all of the ways I continually fail Him. In the same way, I am also to be patient and forgiving of others when they fail to meet my standard of conduct. The doctor may have had his own family emergency. He may have had a fight with his wife or children and needs to make things right before he can concentrate on his patients' needs. Whatever the reason, waiting can be extra hard on the elderly. We are their advocates, and if they are getting tired or agitated, we must not be afraid to politely ask the nurse or receptionist if there is a place where they can lie down, or request a quiet room where they can wait for the doctor. Most offices are understanding of patient needs and will do all they can to accommodate us and our loved one. Some offices will even allow us to call ahead so they can inform us how long it will be before the doctor can see our loved one. This allows us to remain at home until the last minute. We must be sure to save plenty of time for bathroom needs and getting our loved one to the car. We don't want that last minute to turn into an hour and, as a result, miss the appointment.

We never know when circumstances will occur requiring us to make a choice to be patient and forgiving. My son got married in 2008. My father, who was living with us at the time, flew to Iowa with us for the wedding. He survived the trip, as well as the festivities, with his usual jovial spirit. He loved being a part of the wedding. We were able to rent a wheelchair from a local medical supply store and return the chair after the weekend. This was an effective alternative to carrying his wheelchair from one connector flight to another.

Following the marriage celebration, my husband, daughter, father, and I flew back to South Carolina. We made it to Cincinnati, Ohio, where we had to change planes. Unbeknownst to us, my father was not drinking enough fluids because he was afraid he would have to go to the bathroom and possibly miss the next flight. We sat at the gate waiting to board, and I noticed he was getting more and more lethargic. He also became nauseated. From previous experience, I recognized his nausea and lethargy as signs that Dad was about to pass out or have another TIA—a small stroke.

This was not the first time we had dealt with dehydration. We had determined that Dad had not been drinking enough water when he was living alone, because the walk from the living room to the bathroom was too far. This was the primary reason we eventually moved him in with us. We, as caregivers, need to monitor our loved ones' fluid intake and encourage them to drink. We may also need to be available to help them with the toilet.

Back to the airport incident, they called for us to board, and we pushed Dad's wheelchair down the ramp. At the end of the boarding ramp was an elevator to lift my dad and me up to the airplane door, but we had to stand up to use it. I helped my dad walk onto the elevator, and as it began going up, I felt Dad going down. He passed out and I was forced to lay him down in the plane entrance. He could only be described as "death warmed over," and the flight attendants were terrified. One of the flight attendants grabbed the portable defibrillator, looked at me, and said, "It's okay. I'm a mortician, too."

I was momentarily stunned! Then, I saw her place the defibrillator paddles on his chest. "Stop!" I yelled. "He is a no-code. My husband is a doctor and I am a nurse! Get my husband up here and don't do anything." For reason of explanation, a no-code means do not resuscitate in the event of a major, non-reversible heart attack or stroke. We had previously discussed this subject with my dad, and he had signed a living will. Please see also Appendix B—Medical Terminology.

One of the attendants called for the ambulance, and the paramedics came and transported Dad to the hospital. My husband rode in the ambulance and stayed with him until my daughter and I arrived. The gate attendants were amazing. They gave us taxi vouchers to get to the hospital, in addition to food vouchers and hotel vouchers for the night. They also booked us on two separate flights for the next day, hoping we would be able to make one or the other of those flights. As I watched the ambulance drive away, I was not sure if my dad would make it or not. I asked the gate attendants what to do and whom to contact if he did not survive the night. They were so helpful with phone numbers and suggestions. I will forever be grateful for the help they gave us.

After making all the arrangements at the airport, my daughter and I arrived at the hospital to find my father recovering nicely in the emergency room. The physician thought it would be best to admit Dad overnight for observation. I credit Dad's fast recovery to the fact that the paramedics had started Dad on an IV, and as soon as his fluids were replenished, he revived.

What does this story have to do with forgiveness? Well, if my husband had not been with my dad in the hospital emergency room, I am not sure he would have received any care. He did not see a doctor for several hours, and even then, the emergency room doctor did not touch my dad, did not listen to his heart, and did not speak directly to him. The physician merely listened to what my husband said was wrong with Dad and then proceeded to admit him to a bed on the second floor. After we got Dad settled in a room and knew he was going to be okay, we all went to a hotel and got some much needed rest.

We arrived back at the hospital at 9 a.m. only to find my dad very frustrated. He had not had breakfast, nor had he received his morning medicine. Nothing had been done for him!

I was upset but determined to stay calm at that point. I found a nurse who said the doctor had not been by yet to write any orders. Dad could not eat nor have his medicine until the physician had written an order for both Dad's diet and his medication. By then , my father had been in the hospital for approximately sixteen hours, *and no doctor had seen him!* I asked the nurse when the doctor was expected to make his rounds. She had no idea. I suggested she page the on-call doctor to see my father immediately. She appeared to be offended, but I was my dad's advocate at that time.

Thirty minutes later there was still no sign of a doctor. Since Dad was doing well by then, I again found a nurse and requested she get the doctor *at once* and discharge my father, because we had a plane to catch. In addition, Dad needed his pain medicine, and although it was against hospital policy, we gave it to him. We did not have time to wait for the doctor and the subsequent wait for the pharmacy to deliver Dad's medicine. (I do not recommend this approach, by the way.) Finally, a doctor saw my dad and agreed to discharge him immediately. The nurse's understanding of the word "immediately" and my understanding of the same word were apparently quite different. I got my dad dressed, found a wheelchair, rolled him past the nurses' desk, and told them we were leaving to catch our plane. Needless to say, the nurses jumped up and tried to talk us into returning Dad to his room.

"We are leaving. You are welcome to walk us out if you like," I replied.

At the time, I felt justified in treating the hospital staff in such a hostile manner. After all, I was acting as my father's advocate. We got my dad home and after several days of extra rest, he recovered. I did not recover as quickly. I was livid over the treatment we did not receive, and I fired off a letter to the hospital administration. As time passed with no response from the hospital except a bill for services, I harbored an unforgiving spirit. I eventually realized that I had a choice to make. The nurses and doctors were probably understaffed, and it was likely they were doing the best they could under the circumstances. I could either let the anger turn to bitterness and allow the seed of unforgiveness to take root, or I could choose to forgive.

Please do not misunderstand me. We should never overlook maltreatment, mistakes, or the neglect of our loved one. However, we can and should address others in a kind and respectful manner. I was too hasty and demanding at the hospital. I merely wanted to get Dad out of there and get home. My display of irritability and my unforgiving spirit brought shame to the name of Christ, and left no opportunity for a Christian witness.

Who and what else are we supposed to forgive? How about our stubborn siblings, selfish spouses, callous children, church family, and offenses of our childhood? We may need to forgive the offenses of last week, and we may also need to forgive the offense that happened just moments ago.

Do you tend to rehash offenses? Have you ever started a conversation with your husband that went something like this, "Do you know what she had the nerve to say to me this morning?" Proverbs 19:11 reminds us: "The discretion of a man deferreth his anger; and it is his glory to pass over a transgression." We need to let our anger go by asking for God's strength to forgive.

How can we forgive in a Christ-like manner? What are our responsibilities in forgiveness, and what is God's part in forgiveness? God's forgiveness for us is in direct relationship to our willingness to forgive our brother from our heart as stated in Matthew 6:14-15: "For if ye forgive men their trespasses, your heavenly Father will also forgive you: But if ye forgive not men their trespasses, neither will your Father forgive your trespasses." God's part in forgiveness is found in Psalm 103:12: "As far as the east is from the west, so far hath He removed our transgressions from us." East never meets West, so God removes our sin completely. Just as God forgives us completely, and does not remember our sin of unforgiveness, so should we forgive completely. Is it easy? Absolutely not! Is it required as a Christian caregiver? Absolutely!

How many times do we have to forgive? Matthew 18:21-35 states:

> Then came Peter to him, and said, Lord, how oft shall my brother sin against me, and I forgive him? till seven times? Jesus said unto him, I say not unto thee, Until seven times: but, Until seventy times seven. Therefore is the kingdom of heaven likened unto a certain king, which would take account of his servants. And when he had begun to reckon, one was brought unto him, which owed him ten thousand talents. But forasmuch as he had not to pay, his lord commanded him to be sold, and his wife, and children, and all that he had, and payment to be made. The servant therefore fell down, and worshipped him, saying, Lord, have patience with me, and I will pay thee all. Then the lord of that servant was moved with compassion, and loosed him, and forgave him the debt. But the same servant went out, and found one of his fellowservants, which owed him an hundred pence: and he laid hands on

> him, and took him by the throat, saying, Pay me that thou owest. And his fellowservant fell down at his feet, and besought him, saying, Have patience with me, and I will pay thee all. And he would not: but went and cast him into prison, till he should pay the debt. So when his fellowservants saw what was done, they were very sorry, and came and told unto their lord all that was done. Then his lord, after that he had called him, said unto him, O thou wicked servant, I forgave thee all that debt, because thou desirest me: Shouldest not thou also have had compassion on thy fellowservant, even as I had pity on thee? And his lord was wroth, and delivered him to the tormentors, till he should pay all that was due unto him. So likewise shall my heavenly Father do also unto you, if ye from your hearts forgive not everyone his brother their trespasses.

Seventy times seven does not mean I can forgive 490 times, but when I reach 491, I do not have to forgive anymore. Our responsibilities are to show compassion, kindness, humility, gentleness, and patience. We are to bear with grievances, put on love, and minister to the spiritual as well as the practical needs of our loved ones. We are to commit to always keep the other person's best interests in mind. We do this through our actions, thoughts, tongue, and intent. This is impossible to accomplish apart from God's Word and God's help!

God's part in forgiveness is to change the heart, mind, and actions of the person I am responsible for forgiving. Psalm 51:10 tells us: "Create in me a clean heart, O God; and renew a right spirit within me." Notice, it is God's responsibility to change my heart. It is His responsibility to change the other person's heart, too. Although both hearts may be changed at the same time, each act is separate and each is God's job. It is God's responsibility to convict of sin, and meet the spiritual need for love, pardon, and acceptance. God will work out the details of inequity in our sinful lives and this sinful world:

> A new heart also will I give you, and a new spirit will I put within you: and I will take away the stony heart out of your flesh, and I will give you a heart of flesh. And I will put my spirit within you, and cause you to walk in my statutes, and ye shall keep my judgments, and do them (Ezekiel 36:26-27).

Our attitudes concerning forgiveness will reflect in the way we respond to those entrusted into our care. We can have an attitude of compassion: "I do what I do because I love my dad and want to compassionately care for him and show him the love of Christ." In contrast, we can have an attitude of indifference: "I do what I have to do, because I have to do it." In the latter case, we do not willingly take on this responsibility. We will do it grudgingly and brusquely, while refusing to forgive past offenses.

We can have an attitude of kindness or an attitude of tolerance. I readily cared for my dad, but I merely tolerated his slowness. He had three speeds: slow, slower, and slowest. Actually, Dad said his three speeds were slow, slower, and reverse. That was so true! I knew every time I took Dad his meals, he was going to have to use the bedside commode before he would eat. I knew this need, and still I had to choose every time whether I was going to have an attitude of kindness and patience, or simply tolerate it. I had to learn to take Dad his food before I called the rest of the family to the table. If I called the family to the table, and then took Dad his food, they would have eaten and been ready for dessert by the time I finished getting him settled to begin eating. I chose to be kind, I chose to plan ahead, and I chose how to work the situation to best accommodate the entire family. Is it easy to make the adjustment? No, it is not easy, but it is worth learning the lesson to be kind, not just tolerant.

We can have an attitude of gentleness or harshness. My father pointed out to me one day how my voice changed when I got annoyed or impatient. I have a different tone when I want things done my way and now! We need to listen to how we come across in our tone of voice as well as our facial expression and body language. Someone once asked, "What do we do when our parent acts like a child?" I thought for a split second and replied, "We treat them with respect." They are not our children, they are our parents and by virtue of that position we must treat them with respect and gentleness, not harshness. We are not responsible for training our parents; we are only responsible for training our children. By the same token, remember that we are ultimately training the next generation to take care of us someday. We need to model a good example of respect and gentleness while caregiving in front of our children!

We can have an attitude of patience or annoyance. Annoyance comes naturally from our sin nature, but God requires patience. How often have we heard it said, "If we pray for patience, be prepared for God to place us in a situation that is going to test our patience"? Caregiving is the perfect scenario to learn patience and to have it tested. Linda C. shared the following:

> Patience is the ultimate response in caregiving. Patience is also the ultimate struggle in caregiving. It means answering the same question multiple times in a row with a loving tone of voice each time. It means listening to a backseat driver give you directions to a place you have been to on dozens of occasions. It means allowing your elderly parent to help you with a task that will cost you more time to redo and correct afterwards, than if you did it yourself at the beginning. Dare I pray for patience? The only thought that keeps me sane is that someday my own children will be my caregivers, and if I have the

> presence of mind to do so, I will pray to God that they have patience with me.

We can have an attitude of love or an attitude of self-service. Are we caring for our parents or grandparents or even our children because we love them, or merely out of a sense of duty? How we treat our parents, and how our parents treat us, affects the entire family. Linda C. tells the following story:

> Grandchildren are affected deeply by the changes that occur in the lives of their grandparents who are struggling with the maladies of aging. My husband and I were at home discussing the recent decline of his mother's health, when I found my daughter crying in her bedroom. I gently asked what was bothering her. "I miss the old granny," she revealed. I immediately knew what she meant. Dementia not only causes physical and mental changes, but personality changes, too.

The "old granny" could no longer play board games with her grandchildren or remember to send a birthday card or offer a bowl of ice cream during visits. Happy conversations and fun teasing gave way to sullenness and depression. Caregiving affects not only those with hands-on responsibilities, but it also reaches to the youngest hearts — those who crave connection with the person who is no longer there.

While we may feel we have justified reasons for not forgiving others, do we really? As caregivers, we are in danger of developing tunnel-vision. Sometimes we are so busy we cannot see much past our immediate surroundings. We may feel our siblings should be more helpful and not leave the caregiving solely to us. Other times we may become angry when our church family does not meet our expectations. My own church went through a pastoral transition at one point during my caregiving days. I struggled with the lack of a pastor. Our church had no pastor to visit the homebound once a month, and our deacons did not step up and take over that much-needed ministry. However, as I look back, those were my expectations. The church family had many other needs to meet, and they were doing the best they could during this difficult transition. Whether toward an individual or a body of believers, we may need to get our heart right and seek God's forgiveness for an unforgiving spirit. This may require that we go to an individual or even an entire church body and ask for forgiveness.

There may be a time when we are asked to forgive the offenses of our childhood. We may have come from a home in which a parent abused us either physically or mentally. Now, we are being asked to care for that very same parent.

"Whoa! Time out! Care for them? Never!" we may respond vehemently.

Please remember that while we may not have the desire to care for a once abusive parent, the goal of every committed Christian is to become more like Christ. Does Christ expect us to forgive? Absolutely!

How does Christ forgive?

> I will remember their sins no more (Jeremiah 31:34; Hebrews 8:12; Hebrews 10:17); I will pardon their iniquities (Jeremiah 33:8); if they hear, I will forgive (Jeremiah 36:3); I will forgive their sin and heal their land (2 Chronicles 7:14); if you forgive others' transgressions, your heavenly Father will forgive you (Matthew 6:14); blessed is the man whose sin the Lord will not reckon against him (Romans 4:8); so far he has removed our transgressions from us (Psalm 103:12).

The path to forgiveness in an abusive situation is not easy. Donna H. shares her journey from abuse to anger, from anger to hatred, and then finally to choosing, with God's help, to let go of the hatred and forgive:

I am one of three kids, and our lives have been and always will be affected by the day my alcoholic, abusive dad killed my mom. I still find it interesting that my dad's actions had such an impact on so many other lives as well. My mom's family was devastated and never the same. My dad's family was ashamed and didn't know how to handle it. My immediate family went in different directions. My siblings were old enough to live on their own, but I was twelve and had to live with different relatives until I was old enough to live on my own.

My dad went to prison and was released after many years. For me to forgive him was very challenging. I had to forgive him for being an alcoholic, for being physically abusive, and for killing my mother. Trying to forgive without the Lord's help was like falling into a bottomless pit—a pit in which there was no end to the betrayal, hurt, and shame that I felt. Only after I was saved, did I come to realize Christ had adopted me, and I was His child. My Heavenly Father would never let me down or leave me the way my earthly one did. "and, lo, I am with you always, even unto the end of the world. Amen" (Matthew 28:20b).

Even as a Christian, I reached the point in which anger and bitterness were eating at me like a cancer. I began to realize how my dad's actions had spilled onto me, and I was not going to be the person the Lord wanted me to be if I didn't deal with this.

I had an arm's length relationship with my dad when he got out of prison and up until his death. Over these 51 years, God sent many godly women along my path. Two were sixth grade teachers who told me about forgiveness from the Lord and His command for us to do the same. Another was an older lady at church who was a godly example for me when I was in my mid-twenties. In addition, there are several godly women who have been my friends since my forties. I know that's not an accident. The Lord knew what I needed and when I needed it. Without the Lord's help and a lot of prayer, Bible study, and counsel from my godly friends, who I call my extended family, I could not have forgiven my father. He never admitted what he had done, nor did he ask for forgiveness. I pleaded with the Lord for understanding about what had happened and how I could move forward. The answer came back clearly, "Forgive."

Does this mean we must forget? No, it means with Christ's help I can forgive and live in His grace every day. I took a leap of faith that through Him it could be done, and it was completed. Afterwards, I felt as though someone had lifted a car off of my back. Pure joy began to replace anger and bitterness. That joy began to spill out in all areas of my life. "But the fruit of the Spirit is love, joy, peace, longsuffering, gentleness, goodness, faith, meekness, temperance: against such things there is no law" (Galatians 5:22,23).

My father was in a nursing home for a few years before he died. I didn't visit a lot because I was still afraid of him. But one day the Lord opened a door I thought I had closed long before, and with that opening God finished what He had begun in me. I hadn't realized I was still angry and that I still needed answers—like the reason my father killed my mom and why he wouldn't control himself. When I went to the nursing home that day, all I saw was a sad man with dementia whose body did not work anymore.

One day the Lord gave me and other family members closure. There my father lay in a hospital dying. I wanted to pinch him on the arm and ask him if he knew how much pain he had caused. As quickly as the thought came, the Lord replaced it with peace. My dad was unresponsive when I got to the hospital until I touched his hand and he squeezed mine back. I told him I loved him and that I forgave him and that the Lord would too, if only he would ask. I never got to say "goodbye" to my mom, and that had always bothered me. It was overwhelming to see how the Lord worked out every detail—a day to say "goodbye," some closure, and two of his sisters showing up before he died so I did not have to be there alone.

I saw the Lord work even at my father's memorial service. A couple of weeks after my dad died, his sister's husband, who was a fine Christian man, sent me a card saying he believed my dad had accepted Christ some time earlier. That was a blessing I was not expecting. My initial reaction was not expected either—I praised the Lord and then I was angry that he got to go to heaven and be with my mom. I was quickly reminded that I, too, am a sinner, saved by grace—grace I did not deserve. And again God's peace returned. The Lord is willing and totally able to help you, but you have to let Him. "And the peace of God, which passeth all understanding, shall keep your hearts and minds through Christ Jesus (Philippians 4:7).

> Do I still get angry sometimes? Of course. I'm human. I ask myself, do I deserve forgiveness? No, but the Lord gives it. Good can come from evil. "And God is able to make all grace abound toward you; that ye, always having all sufficiency in all things, may abound to every good work" (2 Corinthians 9:8).

Remember, the goal of caregiving is to show love to everyone else, while giving GOD the work of changing MY heart. While it is usually easier to forgive when we do not let anger fester, long-term offenses in which we suffered such things as abuse are not quite as easy. Caregiving, even to those who have hurt us deeply, begins with a choice—the choice to forgive.

-5-

Boundaries

"This is *my* house and I will do what I want, when I want, and how I want! This is *my* kitchen, and I am not your short-order cook! This is *my* dining room table and not yours to take over! This is *my* time, and you are interfering! This is *my* conversation. Stay out of it!"

The word "boundaries" immediately conjures up negative thoughts, but boundaries also provide balance in a somewhat chaotic life. When my mother-in-law, Margaret, moved into our house, my father was already living downstairs. We moved her into my son's old room upstairs, and she immediately immersed herself into our daily lives.

Margaret was the perfect "Southern lady." She would have made a great "mistress of the mansion" had she been born in that era. Her husband ran her bath water for her every morning, made all her meals, did the laundry, and cleaned the house. He accomplished all these tasks because he enjoyed doing them, and it kept him busy. Margaret, on the other hand, played the piano, paid the bills, wrote letters, and made phone calls to friends and family every day. The couple dressed in their best clothes no matter where they went, and they went everywhere together, even to the beauty shop! I always felt that as long as they could take care of each other, it was not necessary for me to be available either for their company or for their pleasure.

One day, my father-in-law fell and broke his hip. A week after surgery, he had a pulmonary embolus (a blood clot to the lungs) and died. After my father-in-law passed away, my mother-in-law continued to live alone, albeit right across the street from my house. She began to have greater difficulty going up and down the stairs inside her house, so we got a physical therapist to come and teach her some exercises meant to strengthen her muscles. The therapist was also supposed to give her tips to help her continue to live on her own.

My mother-in-law never did anything half-way. An "A" on a college course was not good enough; it had to be an "A+." If told to do something, she would do it the best she knew how, as often as she could remember to do it, and better than she had been shown. The physical therapist was unaware of this character trait when she gave Margaret some exercises for flexibility. One such exercise was to stand in front of the kitchen sink and hold on, while stretching the leg backwards, up and down. Due to Margaret's desire to perform the routine correctly, she overdid the stretch and fractured her pelvis. We had her admitted to the hospital and then transferred her to the rehabilitation hospital for physical therapy. This time we made sure the staff understood her willingness to comply with all instructions and the need to watch for signs of over cooperation.

After a week in the rehabilitation unit, Margaret became depressed and unhappy with the unit. She knew that my father was already living with us, felt as though there was no room for her in our home, and assumed she would probably have to stay in the rehabilitation facility until she joined her husband in heaven. I went every day and helped her bathe, went with her to therapy, and stayed most of the day with her. Even so, she was not at home, and she felt unwanted and lonely. She curled into a little ball and gave up. It broke my heart to see her this way. I could not leave her there to die alone at the rehab unit. When I told her we would like her to move into our house, her eyes lit up. She could not believe we wanted her and were willing to make room for her.

I was shocked at how excited and grateful my mother-in-law was to come to our house, and also how much she yearned to be needed. Sadly, I was not as sensitive as I should have been to this need. We moved her into our son's former bedroom, and the fun began. Little did I know that the time had come for the Lord to begin teaching me some powerful lessons concerning selfishness.

Margaret was a great prayer warrior. The first thing she wanted to do when she moved into my house was to spread her journals, her devotionals, and her prayer sheets all over half of my dining room table. I had placed a desk in her room for her to use, but it was not big enough.

Some years prior to this time, Margaret had heart bypass surgery and cardiac rehabilitation. At that time, she was told she needed to walk every day for at least thirty minutes. Fast forward to the time she moved in with us, where she continued walking every day. However, now she walked down my hall, through my dining room, through my kitchen, back down my hall, back up my hall, through my dining room, through my kitchen—all day long! Remember, if told to do a thing once, she tended to do it ten times that amount because more must always be better. This behavior absolutely drove me insane! Because Margaret was the perfect "Southern Lady," we did not correct or question her. Instead, when my dear, patient husband came home from work each day, I would meet him in the bedroom and commence to rant and rave: "Do you know what your mother did today?"

I was the polar opposite of my mother-in-law. It took me a while to realize that I should never put my husband between his mother and his wife. This created a no-win situation for all involved. I remember telling my husband, "John, do not try to solve anything, just let me get it out of my system, and then I will be okay." I did not realize, at the time, what pressure and pain I was causing John by my selfish attitude.

Remember back at the beginning of this chapter where I talked about my house, my conversation, and my kitchen. The Lord in His patient, loving way brought the following thought to mind one day: "Whose house is this?" It caused me to reflect on my outlook concerning belongings. *My* house does not belong to me. It is not *my* dining room table, it is not *my* kitchen, and it is not even *my* hallway. Everything I own belongs to God! He has given me temporary use of these belongings.

This new outlook did not come easily, though. I needed proof, so I had a conversation with God: "Okay, you own everything, but is there a verse in the Bible that tells me this?"

Of course, I should have known there were ample Old Testament verses to prove this important truth. One is found in Exodus 9:29: "the earth is the LORD'S." Deuteronomy 10:14 again solidifies who owns my belongings: "Behold the heaven and the heaven of heavens is the LORD'S thy God, the earth also, with all that therein is." King David in the Psalms also agrees. "The earth is the LORD'S and the fullness thereof; the world, and they that dwell therein" (Psalm 24:1). This same principle is even in the New Testament: "For the earth is the LORD'S and the fullness thereof" (1 Corinthians 10:26). And in case I should miss it the first time, God states it twice in this chapter.

So, who is really the owner of the house we live in and the car we drive? Everything belongs to the LORD and we have the privilege of being His stewards for a short time. If God owns it all, what should our attitude be about His things? Let us take some of the negative issues listed at the beginning of this chapter and see if we can look at them in a positive way, a way more pleasing to the God who owns everything.

EATING

- Negative Reactions

  "Do not tell me what you want to eat. This is my kitchen and I am not your short order cook!"

  Many people lose their appetite as they age. Perhaps they have always eaten their food a certain way, at a certain time, and have cooked it exactly the same for years. My father never wanted to eat but always expected his meals on time. He also did not like to be served left-overs. He much preferred a fresh meal every day. My mother-in-law loved to sit at the dining room table and tell me how to fix her food. It did not matter to her whether it was the same food every day.

- Positive Reactions

  At a time when our loved one's appetite is greatly diminished, they are also dealing with a loss of independence. Be glad they want something specific and are willing to eat anything at all.

ROUTINE

- Negative Reactions

  "I have performed the same routine for the last three months. Yet, when giving you a shower, you still feel the need to tell me what to do every step of the way."

  My mother-in-law loved to take a bath every day. I encouraged her to take a shower only Monday, Wednesday, and Friday as I had to help my dad get his shower on Tuesday, Thursday, and Saturday. Every time I helped either of my parents, they felt the need to tell me what they needed next in the process. I knew what the next step was and resented being told what to do each and every time.

- Positive Reactions

  When helping with activities of daily living, the elderly need to feel the process is their idea not merely our routine. When they begin to tell us how to do something again and again, we need to be patient and hold our tongue. Let them feel they are in control of their daily activity. No one likes to be told what to do. We also need to be mindful of our demands on their routine.

CONVERSATION (TALKING)

- Negative Reactions

  "I cannot have an uninterrupted conversation with my own immediate family at meal times," I complained.

  My mother-in-law was a high school teacher of French and

English for forty-two years. As a teacher, she was always front and center of all conversations in the classroom. She continued to want to be the center of attention; she would turn every conversation back to herself or about something she had read or had heard on television. Much to my shame, I got very annoyed and sometimes talked in a softer voice to my husband, so I could tell him about me and my day, and not be interrupted by his mom's desire to talk about herself.

My husband, a family physician, would tell me about his day at work. He would share some of his patients' experiences, especially some of the more interesting diagnoses. His mom would immediately want to know all of the details: their names, where they lived, and what was wrong with them. I would get extremely annoyed and angry, feeling these details were none of her business. My husband did not share names or personal details with me, and he certainly would not share them with his mother. My husband would patiently respond: "Someone I saw in the office today." Then he would change the subject by asking her a question about herself. He exhibited much greater compassion than I did at the dining room table.

- Positive Reactions

  How can we learn to put a positive spin on our perception that someone is monopolizing a conversation? We need to realize that many elderly people have impaired hearing. When our elderly loved ones are asking questions, usually they are not being nosy; they are trying to be included in the conversation. They are trying to understand what is taking place around them. They generally like to talk about themselves, because they can then control the conversation and not get lost in the dialogue.

  Be sensitive to their loss of hearing. Never, ever follow my example of deliberately speaking softer so they do not have to be included. In addition, be careful not to shout at a hearing impaired person. My father could not hear my husband's tone of voice, but he had no problem with the range of my voice. If we lower our pitch, rather than raising our volume level, we may be heard much easier.

CONVERSATION (LISTENING)

- Negative Reactions

  My mother-in-law loved to talk happily in the morning. On the contrary, I am not a morning person. Do not talk to me until I have had my coffee and devotions. Then maybe I will be thinking intelligently enough to have a conversation.

- Positive Reactions

  Use this as a time to acquire a gentle and quiet spirit. We do not have to talk—just listen. Listening can be a great blessing not only for us but also for our loved one. It makes the one we are caring for feel important, and it shows them we care enough to truly listen to what they have to share. We may be amazed at the stories we hear when we are quiet long enough to listen.

EXERCISE

- Negative Reactions

  As I mentioned earlier, my mother-in-law walked constantly. Constant motion drove me nuts.

- Positive Reactions

  How we respond is a choice. Eventually, I let her faithfulness to exercise encourage me to exercise more regularly. She was eighty years old and had exercised faithfully every day for the last thirty years. Surely, I could do the same. Do not use the first part of the verse in 1 Timothy 4:8 as an excuse for not exercising: "For bodily exercise profiteth little: but godliness is profitable unto all things, having promise of the life that now is, and of that which is to come." 1 Corinthians 6:19 and 20 are great verses to memorize and encourage us in our desire to live a life pleasing to the Lord and to be a testimony to those around us:

> What? know ye not that your body is the temple of the Holy Ghost which is in you, which ye have of God, and ye are not your own? For ye are bought with a price: therefore glorify God in your body, and in your spirit, which are God's.

PERSONAL SPACE (BOUNDARIES)

- Negative Reactions

No privacy! When we move someone else into our living space, one of the hardest situations to deal with is the loss of privacy. We initially moved my dad into a spare bedroom downstairs. He could somewhat take care of himself, so we got a small dorm-like refrigerator and set it on a coffee table to make it the right height. We did not want it on the floor, where he would have to bend down to get his food and potentially lose his balance. He was then able to get food in and out for his meals. We also put a small microwave and some dishes in his room. This apartment-like arrangement gave him a sense of independence, but allowed him to be close at hand. I would prepare my family meal and put the leftovers in small containers. Then I would place them in Dad's freezer so he could have a home cooked meal when he wanted it. I also took him to the grocery store to pick out the single serving meals from the freezer section. He especially liked the ham and cheese pocket sandwiches and the stuffed green peppers (something I would never fix fresh). I also placed a small plastic basket in the room for him to put his dirty dishes in after he ate.

On the other hand, we moved my mother-in-law upstairs into the bedroom directly across from ours. Our living room, kitchen, and dining room were all on the same level and our privacy was gone. Margaret wanted to be included in everything. I am sad to say I initially resented this loss of privacy.

- Positive Reactions

Eventually, I became grateful for the fact that at least I was home and not having to constantly run to a nursing home or an assisted living facility every day to provide care for her. I know a number of families who go to the nursing home every day to check on their loved ones and to feed them their meals. I have so much respect and admiration for these faithful family members, who sacrifice their time to be available for their loved ones, many for years at a time.

Three out of the five family members I cared for had to be in the rehabilitation center of the nursing home for fractures at some point in my caregiving journey. Going to the rehabilitation unit every day, day in and day out, is exhausting. I learned to give thanks for staying home with my loved ones.

PERSONAL RESPONSES

- Negative Reactions

Constant compliments can become annoying. At first glance, it would seem that compliments are always appreciated. My mother-in-law never said an unkind word to anyone, ever. I could get up in the morning and come out with no make-up and my hair a mess.

"You look so good this morning," Margaret would say. "Are you using a new make-up? Your face is so beautiful."

"I don't have any make-up on. Leave me alone!" I wanted to respond. Margaret always loved what I was wearing, loved my hairstyle, loved my shoes, loved the food, and loved how the house looked. My dad, on the other hand, gave compliments very sparingly. As a result, I tended to believe his compliments and seldom ever believed hers.

- Positive Reactions

  Enjoy every compliment. They could be constant complaints instead. I never thought I would miss Margaret's constant compliments, but I do miss them now.

PERSONAL ATTITUDES

- Negative Reactions

  Constant Complaints!

  How do we handle someone who complains about everything we try to do for them? Nothing is ever good enough or done the right way. My mother always wanted things done, but they had to be done her way, in her time frame, and at her command. My brother and sister never did anything right. I was her "good girl" and got to hear all the complaints against my siblings. These complaints were difficult to hear, but it also made me feel superior to my siblings. I tried to be the peacemaker between the family members, but I know I did not always handle things correctly. My mother was a constant complainer—so much so, that at one time my husband asked me not to take our children to her house. He did not want them picking up on their grandmother's critical spirit.

  That surely hurt. I finally wrote my mom a letter asking her to work on her attitude and constant criticism, or I would not be allowed to bring the grandchildren to see her. She tried to do better and was actually very loving to my husband and the children, but a life time of critical thinking and speaking is hard to break. I am sorry to say, she died so suddenly that my siblings did not have an opportunity to realize the love she had for them and their children. My father also complained about a lot of things when he moved in with us. Dad never liked the food. It was too hot, too spicy, too bland, too salty, or not salty enough. As I mentioned earlier, he never wanted the same thing to eat two days in a row. Physically, Dad was always too hot or too cold; socially, visitors either stayed too long or no one ever came to visit.

- Positive Reactions

  How do we deal with constant complaints without being affected by the bad attitudes?

  We can only respond to the constant complaints by going to the Scriptures for help. "A soft answer turneth away wrath, but grievous words stir up anger" (Proverbs 15:1).

  At first, I took the complaints personally. Eventually, I learned to let them go in one ear and out the other without allowing them to stop in between. I learned not to respond with my own complaint, and I learned to control my anger when my mom or dad complained. "In the multitude of words there wanteth not sin: but he that refraineth his lips is wise" (Proverbs 10:19). Sometimes we may have to literally hold our tongue (or at least visualize holding it). We can laugh at that odd word picture, but God's word and God's way always works. It is not easy, but meditating on God's word, especially Proverbs 15:1 (as quoted above) is a great help.

  I will say, when moving an additional family member into our home, if at all possible, we need to move them to an area where our normal living space will not be affected. We want our loved one to be within easy reach, but we still have a responsibility to take care of our spouse and our children. Serving and caring for loved ones in our home will take the grace of God found in Acts 20:32:

> And now, brethren, I commend you to God, and to the word of his grace, which is able to build you up, and to give you an inheritance among all them which are sanctified.

It will also require the wisdom of God found in James 1:5:

> If any of you lack wisdom, let him ask of God, that giveth to all men liberally, and upbraideth not; and it shall be given him.

It is a challenge, but God's grace is sufficient:

> And he said unto me, my grace is sufficient for thee: for my strength is made perfect in weakness. Most gladly therefore will I rather glory in my infirmities, that the power of Christ may rest upon me (2 Corinthians 12:9).

At the age of eighty-one, my father memorized James 3:17. I think it is a good way to end this chapter. I challenge us to also memorize and heed it daily:

> But the wisdom that is from above is first pure, then peaceable, gentle, and easy to be intreated, full of mercy and good fruits, without partiality, and without hypocrisy.

We began the chapter discussing boundaries, but we end talking about attitudes. We can and should embrace the privilege of caring for all of our family, including multiple generations.

-6-

Caregiver Burnout

I hear a loud and long "yes," followed by a huge sigh, from most caregivers upon reading the title of this chapter. In 2004, "Evercare Study of Caregivers" by *Caring Today*, reported the following statistical realities regarding caregivers: 17% reported being in fair to poor health, compared to 9% of the general population; 35% say their health is worse due to caregiving responsibilities; 75% said they had no choice in taking on their caregiving role; 9% reported being depressed; and 34% provide care an average of 40 hours per week. Personal prayer was cited by caregivers as offering the most significant solution to their own needs.

After taking care of my mother-in-law and my father at the same time, I periodically needed a break. I had such conflicting emotions. I knew I did not want to be where I was, but neither did I want to be anywhere else. My husband saw what was happening to me. I will never forget the day he told me to drive over to the next town, about thirty minutes away, and spend the day shopping. Yes, he actually told me to go shopping, and he even provided some money to spend. He stayed home and acted as caregiver for the day, while I got in the car and drove away. About ten minutes down the road, I started having a panic attack. I had never had one before, nor have I had one since, but I suddenly began to hyperventilate. I also started to cry as I struggled with confusing thoughts: *I can't do this. I should be home with my dad. What if something happens while I'm gone?*

I almost pulled over to the side of the road and turned around, but in that moment of panic, the Lord in his graciousness brought Philippians 4:8 to mind:

> Finally, brethren, whatsoever things are true, whatsoever things are honest, whatsoever things are just, whatsoever things are pure, whatsoever things are lovely, whatsoever things are of good report; if there be any virtue, and if there be any praise, think on these things.

I began to meditate on that passage. The truth was that my father was being well taken care of by my husband. I knew in all honesty I could trust my husband as a physician to be ready for any emergency. The bright, sunny day was pure and lovely as I drove to the mall for the shopping trip provided by my husband. After taking a moment to reflect on this scriptural passage, I calmed down and relaxed. I continued to the next town and used all of my spending money. I came back refreshed, happy, and ready to resume my role as a caregiver.

SYMPTOMS OF BURNOUT

If we as caregivers experience any of the following symptoms, we may be suffering from burnout:

- Gradual withdrawal from friends or family
- Decreased interest in activities—tennis, church, club meetings, regular times of attendance at specific events we have once enjoyed
- Feeling blue, irritable, helpless, or hopeless
- Changes in appetite
- Weight loss or gain

- Sleep disturbances: either the inability to sleep or sleeping all of the time

- Increased incidences of personal illness

- The dangerous progression of burnout may ultimately manifest itself with a desire to hurt ourselves or the person for whom we are caregiving. The news frequently shares stories of elder abuse. On March 7, 2011, CNN reported the testimony of actor Mickey Rooney regarding his own elder abuse by his stepchildren.

> For years I suffered silently. I didn't want to tell anybody. I couldn't muster the courage and you have to have courage. I needed help and I knew I needed it. Even when I tried to speak up, I was told to shut up and be quiet.[3]

Unfortunately, the incidence of verbal and physical abuse crosses all racial, socioeconomic, and religious boundaries. If you should ever get to the point at which you entertain the thought of hurting either yourself or someone you are caring for, you should seek help immediately. You need to call a friend or your pastor, and ask them to come over and honestly talk with you regarding your current situation. You are not alone, and it is not unusual for the long-term caregiver to at some point wish it was over.

Let us return to the lessons God needed me to learn from my mother-in-law. When we brought my mother-in-law home from the rehabilitation hospital, I said to my husband, "I cannot let her die there all alone. We should move her in upstairs, and love and care for her during her last weeks on earth."

Well, she thrived in our home not for a few weeks but for an additional six months. At one point I said to someone, much to my shame today, "She just won't die!" I had reached my breaking point and was exhausted. I wanted out of the situation. Below, Linda C. shares the burnout moment that happened early in her caregiving journey:

> Early on in the diagnosis of dementia in both Dad and Mom, I took it upon myself to be the coordinator of all family communications. Because I am a can-do person, I reveled in collecting information from various family members and neighborhood friends. I busily coordinated doctor visits, gave dietary suggestions, and kept family members informed.
>
> As Dad's and Mom's conditions worsened, I became increasingly burdened down with negative responses from family members and my husband's lack of handling the problems on my timetable. I quickly learned that my place as a daughter-in-law was to support and help my husband. When I directed emails and calls his way, he was better equipped to handle the pressures and make important decisions involving his parents and their care.
>
> Learn your place in the caregiving spectrum and be content to function in that position. I now take joy in supporting my husband through prayer and encouragement in a less active and more supportive role.

It is easy to become depressed and overwhelmed. So, how do we overcome our burnout phase? I would like to share what helped me during those special times.

MONITOR OUR THOUGHTS

Remember Philippians 4:8-9, "Finally brethren, whatsoever things are true . . . think on these things." Keeping our mind focused on what is true, what is honest, and what is lovely is much easier said than done, but with God's help we can choose to think on things that are just, pure, and lovely. We do not need to let the "what ifs" keep our thought life in turmoil. We must never doubt God's ability to control and sustain us during this trial.

MEDITATE ON GOD'S WORD

God's Word is rich with words of encouragement. Psalm 1:2 is an exhortation to meditate on His word: "But his delight is in the law of the Lord and in His law doth he meditate day and night." God also gives us many examples of those who were discouraged and how He met each one on an individual basis. Remember the example of Elijah in 1 Kings 17:1-6:

> And Elijah the Tishbite, who was of the inhabitants of Gilead, said unto Ahab, As the Lord God of Israel liveth, before whom I stand, there shall not be dew nor rain these years, but according to my word. And the word of the Lord came unto him, saying, Get thee hence, and turn thee eastward, and hide thyself by the brook Cherith, that is before Jordan. And it shall be, that thou shalt drink of the brook; and I have commanded the ravens to feed thee there. So he went and did according unto the word of the Lord: for he went and dwelt by the brook Cherith, that is before Jordan. And the ravens brought him bread and flesh in the morning, and bread and flesh in the evening; and he drank of the brook.

Elijah had the care of an entire nation on his shoulders against the anger of King Ahab, Queen Jezebel, and probably many of the citizens of the country. He was running and hiding in fear. Yet, God in His mercy and love brought Elijah to a cave where he found rest and a refreshing cool stream to satisfy his thirst. God even sent ravens to supply food for Elijah and replenish his physical needs. How can we doubt God will meet our needs today as we study what He did for His servants in the Scriptures? Elijah's story continues in 1 Kings 17:7-16:

> And it came to pass after a while, that the brook dried up, because there had been no rain in the land. And the word of the Lord came unto him, saying, Arise, get thee to Zarephath, which belongeth to Zidon, and dwell there: behold, I have commanded a widow woman there to sustain thee. So he arose and went to Zarephath. And when he came to the gate of the city, behold, the widow woman was there gathering of sticks: and he called to her, and said, Fetch me, I pray thee, a little water in a vessel, that I may drink. And as she was going to fetch it, he called to her, and said, Bring me, I pray thee, a morsel of bread in thine hand. And she said, As the Lord thy God liveth, I have not a cake, but an handful of meal in a barrel, and a little oil in a cruse: and, behold, I am gathering two sticks, that I may go in and dress it for me and my son, that we may eat it, and die. And Elijah said unto her, Fear not; go and do as thou hast said: but make me thereof a little cake first, and bring it unto me, and after make for thee and for thy son. For thus saith the Lord God of Israel, The barrel of meal shall not waste, neither shall the cruse of oil fail, until the day that the Lord sendeth rain upon the earth. And she went and did according to the saying of Elijah: and she, and he, and her house, did eat many days. And the barrel of meal wasted not, neither did the cruse of oil fail, according to the word of the Lord, which he spake by Elijah.

God not only met Elijah's needs at just the right moment, but he also met a woman's desperate needs at the exact same time. Both were asked to trust God in a very difficult situation. God does not always take away our trials, but He is with us and will provide for us in our hour of need just as He did for Elijah and the widow. Lamentations 3:22-24 speaks of God's faithfulness:

> It is of the LORD's mercies that we are not consumed, because his compassions fail not. They are new every morning: great is thy faithfulness. The LORD is my portion, saith my soul; therefore will I hope in him.

LISTEN TO SOOTHING MUSIC

Television is company, but music soothes and does not require our full attention. "Sing unto the Lord with Thanksgiving" (Psalm 147:7a). Sitting together and listening to the old hymns can provide a special time of bonding. Taking care of someone who can't communicate can make a caregiver feel lonely and depressed. Music has been shown to engender a response, and may even spark an interest in those with dementia. Music from long ago will bring back memories and may calm not only our heart, but also the heart of our loved one.

SHOW KINDNESS JUST BECAUSE!

God commands us to love each other. It is sad to realize that God has to command us to love. However, during the long days and nights of caregiving, we may have to cling to the command to love our family members. We may be tired and our temper may be right below the surface ready to blow up over the slightest offense. Even when we are at our lowest, God commands us to demonstrate Ephesians 4:32, "Be ye kind one to another, tenderhearted, forgiving one another, even as God for Christ's sake hath forgiven you."

WATCH A FUNNY MOVIE

Laugh merely for the fun of it. When we can laugh at our circumstances instead of crying, we have made substantial progress: "A merry heart doeth good like a medicine" (Proverbs 17:22a).

DIET AND EXERCISE

Diet and exercise are important because they help keep both our physical and emotional well-being intact. We need to eat, drink, and stay fit in order to fulfill our tasks at maximum capacity. Exercise increases our endorphins—our feel-good hormones. It not only improves our physical stamina but also our emotional stamina.

> What? Know ye not that your body is the temple of the Holy Ghost which is in you, which ye have of God, and ye are not your own? For ye are bought with a price: therefore glorify God in your body, and in your spirit, which are God's (1 Corinthians 6:19-20).

The reason for maintaining a healthy diet, portion control, and regular exercise is to glorify God in our actions and attitudes. We need to remember to take care of ourselves in the process of caring for others. One of the ways we accomplish this is by maintaining good, healthy eating habits. We also need to make time for some intentional exercise, at least thirty minutes a day, even if we have to break it up into three ten-minute sessions. 1 Corinthians 10:31 is a well-known verse that sums it up for us: "Whether therefore ye eat, or drink, or whatsoever ye do, do all to the glory of God."

God's desire for us is to not just endure our trials, but to lean on Him and trust Him with our lives and the lives of our loved ones as each trial manifests itself.

-7-

Independence Versus Dependence

From the day we are born, we are taught to grow up, go to school, get a job, get married, and have a family; but we are not taught how to grow old. We spend our whole lives learning to live independently, but when we are suddenly faced with the possibility of returning to dependence, our years of training are no longer applicable. Our sense of accomplishment fades, and we begin to wonder why we are still here on earth. My father's reaction was typical of so many others. He wondered why God was taking so long to call him to heaven since Dad felt he had nothing left to offer. Caregivers wonder why God does not take their demented parent home when they do not know what they are doing, where they are, or even who the family member is who is caring for them. Linda C. relates this story:

> When Dad died, a large part of Mom disappeared from this present world. Her foremost desire in this life is to enter the next and be with her husband again. For those of us yet living, it is difficult to process the thought that our loved one may be thinking of suicide. In brighter years, I remember sitting on the porch listening to Dad and Mom give strict instructions not to allow excessive medical measures to sustain their lives in the event of catastrophic tragedy or illness. But when Mom asked if she would die by not taking her medications (statin, blood pressure,

> anti-depressant), we used the threat of her possibly suffering a stroke and sustaining a vegetative state against her.
>
> She continues to take her pills so as not to become a burden to others. We smile at the small victory in this battle for the will to live, but the struggle can become a selfish one on the part of the caregiver. Can I compassionately try to understand my parent's desire to be with Jesus instead of suffering here on earth? Or do I selfishly desire to keep them with me so I do not have to walk through the valley of the shadow of death? The answer is not an easy one for those involved.

Proverbs 3:1-6 talks about long life, and encourages us not to question, but to trust the God who created us for His glory.

> My son, forget not my law; but let thine heart keep my commandments: For length of days, and long life, and peace, shall they add to thee. Let not mercy and truth forsake thee: bind them about thy neck; write them upon the table of thine heart: So shalt thou find favor and good understanding in the sight of God and man. Trust in the Lord with all thine heart; and lean not unto thine own understanding. In all thy ways acknowledge him, and he shall direct thy paths.

I often tell those who have little else to do except sit in a chair or lie in the bed, "You can still pray. Pray for your family, your grandchildren, your church family, your neighbors, your friends, your country, and its leaders; and while you are praying, you can pray for me."

DRIVING

What losses will an elderly person face? While the losses vary from one person to another, the number one response to this question is always the loss of the ability to drive. The next comment goes something like this: "How do I get my mom or dad to stop driving? Their life will be so narrowed down, and I do not have time to take them everywhere they want to go."

As a caregiver, our number one priority is the safety of our family member and those he or she may come in contact with while driving. We may have tried all of the good psychology that others have tried in these situations: "You wouldn't want to hurt someone. You can't see as well at night as you used to see. I will be happy to transport you anywhere you need to go." Sometimes this works and other times it does not. If our loved one still refuses to give up their car keys—and consequently their independence—under no circumstances do we want this to become a source of ongoing conflict and even rage on the part of the elderly driver.

When all else fails, we may need to ask their family physician to send a letter to the highway department. The physician will state that this elderly driver should be given a driving competency exam. The highway department will send our loved one a letter giving a deadline to either come in for an evaluation, or have their license revoked. In all the years my husband has done this for his patients, only two have passed the evaluation. By revoking our loved one's driving privilege in this manner, they will not get mad at us, because the doctor and the Highway Patrol were responsible for the decision. When our loved one rages against these people, we should listen sympathetically. However, we should not offer to intervene or help to get their license back. At this point, we should take the car keys away. When the time is right, discuss what they would like to do with their car. Many times, it helps an elderly individual to more willingly give up their car, if they are giving it to a grandchild or some other person who desperately needs transportation. They may respond to the concept of selling the car to a grandchild and using it as an opportunity to help them learn financial responsibility. They could also be called upon to share their car care experiences and expertise.

GOOD PERSONAL HYGIENE

We may begin to notice that our loved one does not smell fresh, is not wearing clean clothes, or their hair is not styled in the manner we are used to seeing them. We will need to determine if they are developing some dementia, or if they are merely having difficulty getting in and out of the tub. Shower stools, shower chairs, shower bars, shower gel, and scrubbies can help ease the difficulty of bathing or showering.

When I encouraged my mother-in-law to stop taking a tub bath and instead take a shower, she was not happy. Yet, she agreed to try the shower. She eventually enjoyed it and actually felt safer getting in and out of the shower stall. My grandmother refused to take a tub bath or a shower, but kept herself clean by sponging off in the sink. Her generation did this routinely, so it was normal for her. If the cause for poor hygiene is the result of dementia, we may have to intervene regularly. Remember, our loved ones are not exercising every day, so a daily bath may not be necessary.

THE FIVE SENSES

Vision, hearing, taste, smell, and touch may all be affected with age. Changes in vision among the elderly occur in both positive and negative ways. My father had multiple small strokes which temporarily gave him double vision. He needed to cover one eye in order to read his Bible or other books. The problem was annoying, but fortunately it was only temporary.

Cataract removal and lens implants have become so refined, vision among the elderly is sometimes better than it is for younger people. Reading is a wonderful pastime for some older people. With their improved vision, they can read at their own speed, whereas watching TV may be too difficult to follow or hear. I purchased an eBook reader for my father, increased the font size, and he loved reading for a long time.

A favorable aspect of the e-reader is that it is lighter weight than a regular book—a help for those with arthritic hands. It is important to introduce this new device slowly. At first, our loved one may reject the thought that they no longer have a real book in their hands. If we are patient, the e-reader will eventually be the source of renewed reading enjoyment. One advantage to the e-reader is that if our loved one falls asleep while reading, the device will go into hibernation. When they awaken, they will be able to return to the page they were reading, just by turning the switch back on. We must be sure to increase the font size for easier reading.

Loss of hearing is probably one of the most frustrating losses in the elderly. Hearing aids are very helpful, but also very expensive. At this time, Medicare will not pay for hearing exams or hearing aids. I found talking in a lower-pitched voice, rather than a louder voice, was easier for my dad to comprehend. Some voice tones are easier to hear than others. We should not let it annoy us when we are asked to repeat what we said. My husband's tones were not easily understood by my dad, and I would often have to be the interpreter. Be sensitive to the need for an interpreter when others come to visit, too. My father asked me to stay when visitors came, so I could repeat what the visitor said to my father. This made the social calls more enjoyable for everyone.

Like the sense of hearing and sight, the sense of taste also diminishes. Food will taste different from day to day, and eventually nothing may appeal to our loved one's taste buds. This can be frustrating if we do not understand what is happening physically. An excerpt from an article titled, "Loss of Taste in the Elderly," by Marlo Sollitto explains it this way:

> The taste cells are clustered within the taste buds of the tongue and roof of the mouth, and along the

lining of the throat. Many of the small bumps that can be seen on the tip of the tongue contain taste buds. At birth, we have about 10,000 taste buds scattered on the back, side, and tip of the tongue.

After age 50, we may start to lose taste buds. We can experience five basic taste sensations: sweet, sour, bitter, salty, and umami, or savory. Umami was discovered by a Japanese scientist in the early part of the twentieth century. It is the taste of glutamate, a building block of protein found in chicken broth, meat stock, and some cheeses. Umami is the taste associated with MSG (monosodium glutamate) that is often added to foods as a flavor enhancer.

The five taste qualities combine with other oral sensations, such as texture, spiciness, temperature, and aroma to produce what is commonly referred to as flavor. It is flavor that lets us know whether we are eating an apple or a pear. Many people are surprised to learn that we recognize flavors largely through our sense of smell. Try holding your nose while eating chocolate. You will be able to distinguish between its sweetness and bitterness, but you can't identify the chocolate flavor. That's because the distinguishing characteristic of chocolate is largely identified by our sense of smell as aromas are released during chewing.

Food flavor is affected by a head cold or nasal congestion because the aroma of food does not reach the sensory cells that detect odors. A distorted sense of taste can be a serious risk factor for heart disease, diabetes, stroke, and other illnesses that require sticking to a specific diet. When taste is impaired,

> a person may change his or her eating habits. Some people may eat too little and lose weight, while others may eat too much and gain weight.[4]

In talking with dieticians who regularly work with the elderly, they have noticed that the taste of sweetness seems to linger the longest. Unless the patient is a diabetic, the dietician sweetens everything they can in order to make the food more palatable. When all else fails, we need to encourage our loved one to eat if for no other reason than it is time to eat. My father liked to drink a hot chocolate flavored protein drink in the morning and pretend it was his coffee. Good quality breakfast drinks or meal shakes are great protein boosters for the not-so-great eaters.

SHORT-TERM MEMORY

Short-term memory may also begin to fade, while long-term memory often sharpens. Short memory lapses can be a source of conflict because we may have to repeat what we need, or where we are going, over and over again. However, older stories (recalled because of good long-term memory) need to be recorded. It would be a great project for our son or daughter to set up a video camera and have several interviews with our loved one. We can encourage the young person to come up with the questions, and make sure we have plenty of time for the answers to be recorded. There is a wealth of information in the memory of the elderly. What a treasure to find it and pull it out for future generations to keep.

As short-term memory fades, so does the ability to comprehend change. Linda C. gives a perfect example of the need to think before making even simple changes:

> It is extremely important in the early stages of dementia that common household tasks remain the same. As Mom struggled to work the TV remote, it did not help that a relative switched cable companies

> to save money on bundling digital services. New directions could not be learned. Mom was not able to understand and work the new TV remote, grasp the concept of the new internet, or manage new features connected with the telephone. In dealing with memory loss, new is not always better.

So, what should our response be to losses our elderly loved ones experience? In addition to what I have already discussed, it is important to hold them responsible for what they are capable of doing. We need to encourage them to move out of their comfort zone, but keep them within their ability zone. We should allow maximum freedom by letting them do for themselves everything they are able to do, as long as it is not harmful to us or to them. This will require the challenging attribute we discussed earlier—patience. It is hard to let them proceed at their own pace. It is hard to let them do things their own way. It is hard to allow them into our domain when we know we could do it much faster by ourselves. We can encourage our loved one to set the table for dinner; let them call everyone to dinner; and let them pray for the meal. We can give them household responsibilities to accomplish. It will go a long way in making them feel useful and wanted. In summary, we should make the task not only meaningful, but also a task that falls within their capabilities.

It is only by relying on the wisdom and grace of God that we can face each day with a renewed sense of His presence. It is only by His power that we are able to show forth a patient, quiet spirit while facing the multitude of tasks before us each day. My father's favorite verse is worth repeating here: "But the wisdom that is from above is first pure, then peaceable, gentle, and easy to be entreated, full of mercy and good fruits, without partiality; and without hypocrisy" (James 3:17).

-8-

End-of-Life Care

End-of-life care runs the gamut from the extreme of euthanasia, to Jack Kevorkian's style of assisted suicide, to the opposite extreme of keeping the body breathing and the heart beating at all costs. This may include feeding tubes, catheters, ventilators, and any number of additional artificial means of support meant to postpone death.

What should be the Christian's viewpoint for loved ones facing the imminent end of life? Unfortunately, there is not a tidy little verse box tied with a ribbon to address specific questions regarding end-of-life care. Not until the 1950s did we have machines capable of forcing air into our lungs and medicines capable of regulating our heart rate and blood pressure. These tools of modern medicine enable physicians to monitor and artificially prolong our basic body functions. End-of-life decisions are not specifically addressed in Scripture, but there are underlying principles we can base our decisions on regarding our loved ones. God has the final say over life and death. Our very being was created by God, for God, and is sustained by God.

Euthanasia is the act or practice of killing or permitting the death of hopelessly sick or injured individuals in a relatively painless way for reasons of mercy. Euthanasia is a deliberate act of killing. The Bible never condones euthanasia.

End-of-life care, while not as clearly defined in the Bible, still requires hard decisions. Does the Bible advocate or condone the withholding of medical treatment when death is imminent? Let us look at three similar instances and then discuss the Scriptural basis for making end-of-life decisions for our loved ones.

Mr. and Mrs. Jones had been married for over fifty years when she entered the neuro-intensive care unit after a massive stroke. She required a ventilator to support her breathing and aggressive intravenous therapy (IV). She also needed multiple medications to control various aspects of her bodily functions. She needed to have blood drawn for lab work at least twice a day. She had a tube that drained her urine. She had patches on her chest to monitor her heart and a blood pressure cuff that took her blood pressure every hour. A monitor was taped to her finger to measure her oxygen saturation. She had a tube in her nose initially to drain her stomach, and a couple of days later, to feed her with liquid tube feedings. Her best case scenario was that she would recover enough to be "alive" in a nursing home. She was treated for seventeen days in the hospital and finally her heart stopped. CPR was performed (which resulted in several cracked ribs from chest compressions) and after about one hour, she was pronounced dead.

A second example of an end-of-life decision occurred with my sister and her husband, Bill. Several years ago he was hospitalized with a severe infection in his legs. This condition led to massive infection in his blood. His lung collapsed, requiring him to be on a ventilator for almost a week. The doctor told my sister that Bill might not be able to breathe on his own, nor would he be able to eat on his own (necessitating a feeding tube). My sister and her sons said no to the feeding tube and requested the ventilator be removed as soon as possible. In previous conversations with both his wife and son, Bill had made it clear he did not want to be kept alive on machines. Several years before this incident, Bill had signed a living will, where those requests were also made clear. Though it was difficult to make the decision to withdraw the ventilator and consequently bring about the very real possibility of death, the family was able to make the decision based upon what they knew Bill would have wanted.

After the ventilator was removed, Bill regained consciousness and survived two more years. Several weeks after his recovery, the family discussed the ventilator decision and Bill said, "You made the right decision."

Bill's situation was unusual. Seldom do family members have the opportunity to confirm, as they did in his case, that they made the right decision. In any event, these discussions need to take place long before there is a catastrophic event.

Another example also occurred in my personal family. My mother taught school on Friday, had a massive stroke on Wednesday, and died on Saturday. The difference in this scenario and the first one was that both my brother and I were registered nurses, and Mother's son-in-law was a medical doctor. Based upon Mother's initial presentation of symptoms and her subsequent total lack of response, it was obvious this was a terminal event. After several days and getting absolutely no response from Mother to anyone or anything, we all agreed: no ventilator, no antibiotics, no critical care, and no intravenous needle sticks.

When my mother had her stroke, initially she had an IV, but it came out accidentally, and the nurse had great difficulty getting it back in. My brother actually was able to restart the IV, but it began to leak again after one day. At this point, there was no response from my mom and no hope of recovery. The doctors and my brother recommended not restarting the IV—it was not doing anything but bringing me a sense of comfort in that we were hydrating and feeding her. At the time, I knew it was the right decision, but I still had guilt with the idea that we were starving her.

After much research and prayer, I now have a better understanding of what happens to the body when the patient is unresponsive and has no hope of recovery. With no brain activity, there is no way for the body to feel hunger or thirst. There have been several studies among prisoners (with brain activity) who have gone on hunger strikes, and who actually experienced a sense of euphoria after a short period of time without food or water.

God knows the length of our days with or without fluids. At this point in the patient's care, most IV fluids and nutrition are given for the sake of the family, not the patient. My mother received comfort care only. We made sure her lips and mouth remained moist by dipping swabs in water and rubbing them on her tongue and teeth. We also used lip gloss to keep her lips moist. We made sure we turned her from side to side every two hours. These were things we did to provide comfort, even though Mom had no sense of pain after her massive stroke. We provided this minimal care to enable us to know we were her caregivers to the end. We would not and did not abandon her in her final days.

In each of the above three cases, the decisions regarding the medical care of each patient was different. None of these instances resulted in the direct euthanasia of the patient. I believe we can agree that euthanasia is wrong. But when it comes to providing comfort for a loved one who is unresponsive and has no hope of recovery, these measures are more for our benefit. We cannot abandon someone in their final hours. Neither do we want to subject them to unnecessary, painful procedures just because we feel a need to do something. All of the decisions discussed above were acceptable.

> And the Lord God formed man of the dust of the ground, and breathed into his nostrils the breath of life; and man became a living soul (Genesis 2:7).

> God that made the world and all things therein, seeing that he is Lord of heaven and earth, dwelleth not in temples made with hands; Neither is worshipped with men's hands, as though he needed anything, seeing he giveth to all life, and breath, and all things; And hath made of one blood all nations of men for to dwell on all the face of the earth, and hath determined the times before appointed, and the bounds of their habitation; That they should seek the Lord,

> if haply they might feel after him, and find him, though he be not far from every one of us: For in him we live, and move, and have our being (Acts 17:24-28a).

As I stated at the beginning of this chapter, our very being was created by God, for God, and is sustained by God.

My mother-in-law had congestive heart failure, and one night we nearly lost her. The next morning she talked about what she had experienced and told me she had seen her parents, her husband, her former pastor, and my mother—all of whom had already died and gone to be with the Lord. She asked me what I thought that meant. God, in his wisdom, had me encourage her with the realization that heaven is just a step away. Margaret and I firmly believed she was at heaven's gate, and it truly was just a step away. After that episode, she had a sense of peace and was no longer fearful of what might happen when the end did come. She knew the God she served every day of her life would be there for the next step—the one that would take her away from this life and into a new life in eternity with God. 1 Corinthians 15:26, and 15:54-56 states it so beautifully:

> The last enemy that shall be destroyed is death. So when this corruptible shall have put on incorruption, and this mortal shall have put on immortality, then shall be brought to pass the saying that is written, Death is swallowed up in victory. O death, where is thy sting? O grave, where is thy victory? The sting of death is sin; and the strength of sin is the law.

Jesus has bought us the victory over death:

> But we see Jesus, who was made a little lower than the angels for the suffering of death, crowned with glory and honour; that he by the grace of God should taste

> death for every man. For it became him, for whom are all things, and by whom are all things, in bringing many sons unto glory, to make the captain of their salvation perfect through sufferings. Forasmuch then as the children are partakers of flesh and blood, he also himself likewise took part of the same; that through death he might destroy him that had the power of death, that is, the devil. And deliver them who through fear of death were all their lifetime subject to bondage (Hebrews 2:9-10, 14-15).

There is no fear of death for the believer. "And God shall wipe away all tears from their eyes; and there shall be no more death, neither sorrow, nor crying, neither shall there be any more pain: for the former things are passed away" (Revelation 21:4). I do not fear death because I am looking forward to that final earthly goodbye, opening my eyes and beholding the face of my Lord.

Death for the believer is wonderful, but for those left behind there is great pain and sorrow. We long to go with them. We heap guilt on ourselves. Did we do enough? What if we had been there sooner? What if . . . ? Let us turn our focus off ourselves and realize "for to me to live is Christ, and to die is gain" (Philippians 1:21). If our loved ones could speak to us today from heaven, they would repeat those words of Paul. 1 Corinthians 5 gives us a correct view of being absent from the body and being present with our Lord in heaven.

It is vital that we have a conversation now with all of our family, both young and old, regarding the level of treatment we desire to have implemented in a catastrophic event with no hope of recovery. This is not an easy conversation to have, but keeping the above statements in mind, it becomes clear what decisions can and should be made. It is important to remember that these decisions are for a catastrophic event with no hope of recovery, not for a terminal illness from which death may or may not be days or weeks away. Our responsibility is to support our loved ones in their decision.

What about organ donation? In the event a loved one is declared brain dead, should a Christian be involved in organ donation? First of all, if we hear the term "brain dead," we can rest assured that specific criteria have been met by the patient. These criteria prove unequivocally that the patient's vital organs are being kept alive solely because of the ventilator and powerful drugs, which help to regulate the heart rate and blood pressure. There also is no brain activity on an EEG.

If a patient is declared brain dead, we may be asked to donate any or all of the following organs: heart, lungs, kidneys, pancreas, intestine, liver, corneas, bones, or skin. At any given time in the United States, over 100,000 people are waiting on transplant lists for an organ. Many may die within a year or two, if they do not receive a transplant. Organ donation is a means of saving another life, while we are losing our loved one. We were able to donate my father-in-law's corneas after his sudden death. Because this is a very difficult and emotional time, the decision to donate is easier for our family if our loved one has made these wishes known ahead of time. In most states, drivers may indicate their desire to be an organ donor by checking an option on their driver's license. This will also give the family some sense of direction during the crisis.

Once we give our consent, the organ procurement agency determines whether age or disease is a factor in the ability to donate. The counselor will ask us for a detailed history in order to establish the efficacy and safety of the organs considered. This questionnaire is like the blood donation form only a bit more extensive. Once we have consented, the financial burden shifts to the recipient. We will be given the opportunity to say goodbye to our loved one before any organs are taken.

The organ donation process usually takes twenty-four to thirty-six hours. During that time, tissues and organs are typed, cross matched and assigned to specific patients. Special operating teams are flown in so appropriate simultaneous retrieval can take place. Afterwards, the body is released to the funeral home. The fact that organs were donated will not be obvious to visitors, and we may hold a regular viewing of the body if so desired.

Whether a couple has been married thirty, forty, or fifty years, the odds are that one mate will have to face the heart-wrenching decisions concerning end-of-life care. You are strongly encouraged to have a heart-to-heart conversation with all of your loved ones, both young and old, concerning end-of-life care. In the fog of grief, it is easy to lose sight of how to make appropriate decisions from a Christ-filled perspective. In fact, whether a person knows the Lord or does not have confidence in eternity, it is never an easy time of decision making.

We should ask our doctor's opinion about the various treatment options. We can ask the nurses, who see these situations on a daily basis, what they would recommend if it were their family member. We should seek support from our clergy, pray about our decision, make our decision, and be confident that we are doing right in the eyes of God. "To everything there is a season, and a time to every purpose under the heaven: A time to be born, and a time to die" (Ecclesiastes 3:1-2a). "Precious in the sight of the Lord is the death of his saints" (Psalm 116:15).

-9-

Caregiving Is Over—Now What?

When we have been responsible for the care of a loved one for weeks or months or years, and that person passes into eternity, we may initially feel a sense of freedom. Yet, while the heavy responsibility of their care is over, the loss hurts deeply—possibly to an even greater degree having been their primary caregiver. From the beginning of time, grief has been an emotion suffered after the death of a loved one. We miss them. We may wish we could die, so we would not have to continue life without them. For every one of his additional years, my father longed to go to heaven and reunite with his wife. The Bible is filled with examples of men and women grieving for their deceased family members:

Abraham for Sarah:

> And Sarah died in Kirjatharba; the same is Hebron in the land of Canaan: and Abraham came to mourn for Sarah, and to weep for her (Genesis 23:2).

Jacob for Joseph, thinking he was dead:

> And Jacob rent his clothes, and put sackcloth upon his loins, and mourned for his son many days. And all his sons and all his daughters rose up to comfort him; but he refused to be comforted; and he said, For I

> will go down into the grave unto my son mourning. Thus his father wept for him (Genesis 37:34-35).

There are also examples of national mourning: Genesis 50:3 tells us that the Egyptians mourned seventy days with Joseph for the death of Jacob. The Israelites mourned the death of Aaron (Numbers 20:29); of Moses (Deuteronomy 34:8); and of Samuel (1 Samuel 25:1). David and the country mourned the death of King Saul's nephew and an army general, Abner (2 Samuel 3:31–32).

In the New Testament, we see the town mourning with the widow who had lost her only son (Luke7:12). Many wept and wailed with the death of Jarius' daughter (Luke 8:41-42, 49-56). Mary and Martha wept for their brother, Lazarus (John 11:31). Many of us can quote John 11:35, "Jesus wept." Weeping is a means of allowing our grief to escape our body and pour out our pain.

In several of the above Scriptures, there is also mention of the word "wailing." In today's culture, we do not see this loud wailing as often, but from personal experience, wailing is also a part of grief, usually done in private.

Other Biblical expressions of grief were exhibited externally by the tearing of either their inner or outer garments:

> And David said to Joab, and to all the people that were with him, Rend your clothes, and gird you with sackcloth, and mourn before Abner. And king David himself followed the bier (2 Samuel 3:31).

Sackcloth was a dark material made from camel or goat hair. Women wore black or somber material:

> And Joab sent to Tekoah, and fetched thence a wise woman, and said unto her, I pray thee, feign thyself to be a mourner, and put on now mourning apparel, and anoint not thyself with oil, but be as a woman

> that had a long time mourned for the dead (2 Samuel 14:2).

Today, grief is also a natural outpouring of our spirit missing our loved one immediately. Our grief is as intense as their rejoicing is in heaven. Recently, two families lost their children, and they have very eloquently put their grief into words. A mother shares her heart with us concerning her young son, Samuel:

> The Lord blessed Tim and I in that he gave us Samuel—a special gift. He turned seven on November 8th and is the sweetest child most have ever known. He always had a smile on his face and captured all who met him with his beautiful blue eyes and curly blonde hair. He also had special needs. He passed away on September 10, 2012, from Leigh Syndrome, a mitochondrial disease. It affected the movement center of his brain, so everything from his fine motor skills to eating had been damaged by this incurable disease.
>
> Samuel had major respiratory trouble. He was not able to talk but spoke volumes with his eyes. He had a Tobii eye gaze computer that he loved! He could not sit up, walk or even hold his head up without assistance. He had surgery in May of 2008 to get a feeding tube because he was not able to eat enough due to poor muscle tone and control, but he did love food!
>
> Samuel taught us and touched our lives more than any other person. He taught us to treasure each moment, to be content in all circumstances, and to put our faith in God through it all. His smile was contagious, his laugh was like music to our ears, and his heart was pure. He loved his family and friends. He

loved music, dancing, snuggles, and kisses. He always wanted to be holding our hand and will forever hold our hearts. Our hearts will never be whole again with Samuel gone, but we rejoice that he is now healed and whole. He is praising our Lord and running on the streets of gold. He is perfect. We praise the Lord for giving Samuel to us for almost eight years and we will treasure each and every memory.

Two weeks ago I was holding my sweet Samuel still. He had taken his last breath at 6:17 a.m. On Sunday afternoon, the Lord had allowed Tim and I to consider that Samuel may be too sick and weak to keep fighting. He had a fever for a while, but Sunday it became very high and nothing was helping to lower it. Tim and I were by his side all afternoon with cold cloths, a little fan, and medication. His little face was so pleasant, but he was miserable. Then his O_2 became so low, we had to put a cannula on his nose, which normally he would not stand, but he felt so bad he didn't care.

Our other children wanted to go to spend the night with their Grammy and aunts, so we let them. Tim and I sat with Samuel in his new bedroom enjoying the cool air conditioner and watching the sun set. Tim asked Samuel if he could see his angel and Samuel turned his head to the right and looked at the corner. I prayed he would have great comfort. He cooled off a little and went to sleep. His breathing started sounding a little better, and we thought (just like at other times) that he may be getting better. We continued his breathing treatments and that seemed to help a little.

Tim made a comfy spot on the couch for Samuel between us and we slept for a little while. Sometime between 1 a.m. and 4 a.m. Sunday morning, Samuel woke up struggling to breathe. His eyes were open, but he was not looking at us in the normal way. A few other things happened that were confusing and hard and we realized his body was not working right anymore. Tim and I tried so hard to stay strong and comfort Samuel throughout the remainder of the night. We sang many sweet songs about heaven and the Lord's comfort and care. We read Bible verses and prayed over and over. We held our young son's hands and snuggled. We had loved him so richly for almost eight years. The last night was also full of our love for him and the rich blessing he was and is to us. As his breathing became slower, we said again his favorite verses, Psalm 23. Tim wanted to play the song "Come to Jesus" for him and us. As that song played, we reassured Samuel that he was about to be healed eternally and would soon be safe in the arms of Jesus. At that very moment Samuel's soul left his body. As parents, we were broken, and we mourned deeply for our precious son.

We held Samuel for a time and then called our dear hospice nurse. We also called our children and other family members. They came and loved on him, and the Lord brought us great comfort on this day that we had all been dreading. We were able to spend a while with Samuel's body, and then we knew it was time. We said that there would be no need for a stretcher. Tim carried Samuel to the hearse awaiting outside. The funeral director said he had never seen anyone do that before and it changed his life. We loved holding our boy and helping him; that was our life. They took him away and we held each other.

Later that night we wanted to view Samuel's body before the children saw him, and that was so very hard for me. The next day I could see the value in seeing him that way. It was just his shell, he was in heaven. It was so hard to look at him in his funeral bed, those beautiful curls and long eye lashes. He was so perfect and peaceful. He didn't look like he was in pain that last night. I am so very thankful that Tim and I were with him the whole time. Every day since, we have tried our best to figure out how to do life with this huge piece missing.

The grief comes in waves. When 9 p.m. comes I still think I need to hook up Samuel's feeding pump. Tim had been in the habit of coming home from work, going directly to Samuel to talk with him and give him a kiss. Now, Tim stops himself. The house is so quiet without his treatments and the noise of his various medical machines. The oxygen is gone. All of his equipment and his things are scattered about, and I'm not sure when and how to move them. And so much more. The kids are sad and miss Samuel, but they are doing better than we expected. Their grief is apparent, but they each express it in their own way.

Tim and I, and all who love Samuel, are missing him and mourning. We feel a hole in our hearts that is so deep the pain is horrible at times. If you ask us how we are doing, we may not answer, because we are sad, but we don't always know if the person asking really wants to know. We do rejoice that Samuel is healed and is in Glory, but it is painful to know we will never see him here again. He was a precious saint and touched so many lives. We will always be thinking about him and missing him—every day.

Today, I am thankful for God's promises that carry us through this new life without Samuel. We know he is in heaven—happy and perfect in Jesus arms. "Yea, though I walk through the valley of the shadow of death, I will fear no evil, for thou art with me; thy rod and thy staff, they comfort me" (Psalm 23:4).

We sang the following song to Samuel many times over the last few months before he died. A friend had sent it and Samuel knew it well. We sang it on his last night and at his funeral. It is Samuel's song:

And on that day
When my strength is failing,
The end draws near
and my time has come,
Still my soul will sing
Your praise unending,
10,000 years and then forever more!
Bless the Lord, O my soul,
Worship His Holy name.
Sing like never before,
Oh my soul, I worship Your holy name.

(Used by permission from the September 21, 2012 blog of Mary Elizabeth C.)

Elizabeth B. lost her twenty-nine-year-old daughter quite suddenly to unknown causes. She shares her memories below:

Our pastor said last night that the death of a child is like a period before the end of the sentence. As I pondered what he said, I realized it is that and more. It is as if you are in the middle of an engrossing, impossible-to-put-down book, but when you turn the page—instead of continuing lines of type—there are simply two words on an otherwise blank page that read: THE END. You find yourself screaming at the author, "What do you mean? This can't be the end! What about the chapter where she calls about the perfect job that she has waited two years to get? What about the one to Grandma or the one where she . . . ? There are so many chapters waiting. How can this possibly be the end?"

> Then you see there are other pages, and so you turn and read "THE BEGINNING". The rest is in a language you cannot, for now, understand but one day . . . So, for now, you close the book, cling to memories of chapters read and wait for that day. "For by grace are ye saved through faith . . . it is the gift of God" (Ephesians 2:8). "Now if we be dead with Christ, we believe that we shall also live with Him" (Romans 6:8).
>
> I love you Amanda.

Death is a separation that leaves us with desperate sadness and profound loneliness. Yet, for those of us who know the Lord, there is also the knowledge that we grieve not as those who have no hope.

> But I would not have you to be ignorant, brethren, concerning them which are asleep, that ye sorrow not, even as others which have no hope. For if we believe that Jesus died and rose again, even so them also which sleep in Jesus will God bring with him. For this we say unto you by the word of the Lord, that we which are alive and remain unto the coming

> of the Lord shall not prevent them which are asleep. For the Lord himself shall descend from heaven with a shout, with the voice of the archangel, and with the trump of God: and the dead in Christ shall rise first: Then we which are alive and remain shall be caught up together with them in the clouds, to meet the Lord in the air: and so shall we ever be with the Lord. Wherefore comfort one another with these words (1 Thessalonians 4:13-18).

The world's model of grief is said to go through seven different stages. The first stage is shock and denial. For the caregiver, this stage has already taken place as they dealt daily with the inevitable decline. The second stage is pain and guilt, and the third is anger and bargaining. By the fourth stage, depression, reflection, and loneliness manifest themselves. The fifth stage is an upward turn followed by reconstruction and, finally, acceptance and hope.

As Christians, we may feel we should not be subject to the world's pattern for grief. Many well-meaning friends come up with all kinds of things for us to do now that we are no longer busy with our caregiving responsibilities. We may try to fill the void ourselves with various activities. We may volunteer at the church, go back to work, clean out the house, or take up a hobby. All of these activities are good, but are they the best?

After a year—sometimes much sooner—well-meaning people may begin to encourage us to be strong, to carry on, and to get over our loss. The length of the process is different for everyone. We cannot let well-meant (but sometimes senseless) comments discourage us on our road to grief recovery. Some have said to wait a year before making any major decisions. The implication is that after a year, the grief will be gone, and we will be able to think more clearly. I contend that grief never goes away completely. It may lessen in intensity, and the waves of grief may get longer and longer between their peaks, but it will always be present.

It has been over a year since the fifth family member for whom I had primary care "graduated to heaven." I have used this term because it seems gentler than saying "they died." After my mother died in 1995, I had to be strong for my grandmother and my father. As each of the five family members died, I did not take time to grieve their passing, because I always had to stay strong for the rest of the family. Looking back, that was a mistake. I strongly recommend taking time and getting away from everyone and everything for a season. It is very important that we allow ourselves time to grieve, time to look at old pictures, time to read old letters (soon it will be old Facebook entries), and time to sift through our memories. Some may need time alone for just a day or two. Others may need several weeks. The key is to face our grief and allow ourselves time to cry when no one else is around. We can cry to God and know He is holding us and supporting us in our grief. He understands our grief.

As a caregiver, we may also struggle with guilt for feeling relieved that our loved one is finally gone. While we miss the person, we may also experience relief that our caregiving responsibilities are over. Do not feel guilty. These feelings are understandable and part of the normal grieving process. When we can hear someone mention our loved one's name and not tear up (inwardly or outwardly), we will know we are now ready for the next phase of our life.

One year after my mother died, I made this journal entry:

> I cried unto the Lord and he heard my cry! I felt His presence mightily lift me up and carry me through the week. Oh, to realize this presence and dwell in His presence continually. I welcome sorrow as my companion for with Him there is closeness and reliance on my Savior.

What a privilege for me to share in this moment with my readers. For those of us facing a loved one's departure, remember *heaven is just a step away*. We can take comfort and rejoice with our loved one who knows Jesus as their personal Savior, for they will soon step away from us and into life everlasting. For those of us facing life without a loved one, it is important to take time to grieve. I learned the hard way; grief cannot be put off forever.

I finally took time to face my grief seventeen years after my mother died, and the intensity was just as strong as the day she died. I drove alone to the beach and rented a hotel room. I had a time of crying, a time of prayer, a time of searching the Scriptures, and a time of isolation. Others may not understand, but we will know when and where we need to get alone with God and take time to grieve. We should embrace this time with God and renew our understanding of 2 Corinthians 12:9:

> And he said unto me, My grace is sufficient for thee: for my strength is made perfect in weakness. Most gladly therefore will I rather glory in my infirmities, that the power of Christ may rest upon me.

Our infirmity at this point may be our grief, but we must allow the Scriptures to uphold us for now, until we meet our loved one again in heaven. God wants only the best for his children, and only He can fill our lives with His best, as we rest completely and wholly on His Word and what He wants us to do next. The stages of grief need to be met with the light of the Gospel, and faced with hope in God, and the ultimate future of serving Him for eternity.

-10-

For Pastors and Church Families

A physician treats the physical needs of an individual; a pastor meets the person's spiritual needs. When someone is in the hospital, their doctor and their pastor are the two people they most want to see. The importance of a person's spiritual and physical needs has been recognized since Bible times. Jesus showed compassion and healed the sick. The Middle Ages produced monasteries where the priests assisted in caring for the sick. Down through the history of hospitals, there has always been a spiritual advisor either on staff, or appointed as a volunteer to visit the sick and provide religious comfort. Even The Lunacy Act of 1890 specifically provided for the appointment of an Anglican chaplain in each mental hospital. People facing the possibility of an imperfect body, subject to frailties, dependence, and ultimately death find themselves seeking both medical and spiritual guidance.

There is also the same sense of longing for spiritual guidance among shut-ins and their caregivers. Caregivers and their family members feel isolated to some degree both spiritually and physically. What should be the role of church leaders and the church family in meeting both of these needs?

First, according to the following Scriptures, God is concerned with the sick, the widows, and the children:

> Pure religion and undefiled before God and the Father is this, To visit the fatherless and widows in their

> affliction, and to keep himself unspotted from the world (James 1:27). And Jesus went about all Galilee, teaching in their synagogues, and preaching the gospel of the kingdom, and healing all manner of sickness and all manner of disease among the people (Matthew 4:23).

Having been both a patient and a caregiver, I developed a very strong understanding of the feeling of isolation and the desire for church leadership to show they care. Both the homebound and the caregiver need to know and feel they are an important part of the church. I believe it is essential for the pastor, elder, deacon, or lay leader to make it a priority to visit those in the hospital every day if at all possible. Most hospital stays are a week or less. It is also crucial for a pastor, elder, deacon, or lay leader to visit the homebound.

When and how should a visit be made? When my mother-in-law was facing heart surgery, her strongest desire before going into surgery was not only to have her family with her, but also to have her pastor (her shepherd) pray with her before she entered the operating room. When possible, the pastor needs to be there to pray with the patient and their family at least thirty minutes to one hour prior to the scheduled surgery time. It is not necessary to spend more than ten to fifteen minutes at the bedside, but it is such a comfort to the patient facing surgery to know their church shepherd cares about what they are facing.

It is very meaningful for either the pastor or the church secretary to call a family member on their cell phone while the surgery is taking place, or just afterward, as the family awaits the prognosis. The wait can be harder on the family than on the person undergoing surgery. The church needs to be sure someone in the church family is aware of the surgery and will be with the family during the wait. Ideally, this may be coordinated by the church secretary.

One of the best gifts I received while various family members were hospitalized was a small basket of snack foods. Flowers are nice, but some of the odors can be strong, and potted plants have to find a spot in the home once the patient is discharged. The snack food basket included chips, chewing gum, cough drops, granola bars, chocolate, bottled water, juice, and fruit. Snacks available from hospital vending machines are expensive, and the basket was a welcome treat.

If a patient is in the Intensive Care Unit, most hospitals will allow a pastor to have the same visiting privileges as the family, and many times there are no restrictions on the time allowed in the ICU. The pastor needs to know what each hospital will allow. When they visit the patient, the pastor needs to remember that hearing is the last sense to go. Whether or not the patient is able to talk, they can hear and appreciate verbal prayer at the bedside. Being in the ICU can be very stressful to the patient, as it is a strange environment with many strange noises. The reminder that God is with them even at this time is vitally important.

If complications arise, or the end of life is near, hospital regulations usually allow for unlimited pastoral access to the patient and their family. Decisions will need to be made for which the family may turn to the pastor for direction. These include: end-of-life and/or life-prolonging measures; organ donation; to continue to treat or to stop treatment; and specific questions and decisions that the family may be facing on any given day. The pastor needs to be familiar with and understand the medical aspects of end-of-life care.

But what about the aging family member who can no longer get out of the house and come to church regularly, or even at all? Does the church family, as well as the pastoral staff, have an obligation to members who are unable to attend church due to poor personal health or a member's caregiving responsibilities? As a caregiver for the last seventeen years, I experienced both support and feelings of abandonment as my church family went through several changes in leadership.

Ideally, a member of the church family needs to visit or at least call the homebound or their caregiver once a week. This cannot be done entirely by the senior pastor. Any member of the church family can and should visit or call weekly. I strongly encourage utilizing the church secretary to coordinate the visitation schedule. There are online calendars to coordinate care and visits (www.carecalendar.com is one example of an online assist for visits as well as other needs).

When visits are made to the homebound, there are two main things to keep in mind: it is not necessary to take food to the family, and it is necessary to keep the visit to a maximum of fifteen minutes. My father talked and told stories as long as the visitor was there, but once they left he would often say, "I thought they would never leave!" He would be totally exhausted after the visit, and would sleep for the next several hours.

We should also be alert to the caregiver's needs. If they walk with us to another room following our visit to the homebound, they may be indicating their own personal need for companionship. Remember, the homebound individual is not the only one that feels forgotten.

Encourage the homebound, the hospitalized, and the caregivers to stay in the Word of God. Have a short Bible study and pray with them. If a Bible study is not feasible due to time factors (as well as patient fatigue), give them an assignment to read and study, and then email or discuss the lesson on the next visit. It is vital to hold the caregiver and their family accountable for the spiritual temperature in the home. It is easy to let it slide, but it can also be a time of enforced quietness and an opportunity to "be still and know that I am God." Take this great opportunity to encourage spiritual growth for both the caregiver and their loved one.

After the death of a family member, does the church family have any obligation to the surviving family? Absolutely! The caregiver is suddenly free and at a loss as to how to occupy their new-found freedom. In the case of a surviving spouse, they are now totally alone. What should they do? I strongly encourage the pastoral staff and church family to continue the once a week visits or calls for the next one to three months, then gradually decrease them to once a month as needed. It is vital the caregiver understands that while their immediate job is done, they are still important to the church family. The caregiver may find it hard to assimilate back into the church family and the various activities. Assigning a church member to be the former caregiver's companion for the first three to six months is very beneficial. Sitting with the surviving spouse so they are not in their church pew alone means the world to them.

Bill H. was married for sixty-five years when his wife died. It was extremely difficult for him to come to church and sit alone. One Sunday, as he sat in the pew listening to the choir, he wondered why God did not take him to heaven at the same time as his wife. Bill felt an overwhelming desire to leave the service rather than be embarrassed by crying. When the choir members came down out of the choir loft, one of the college girls noticed Bill looking lonely and decided to sit beside him. Bill has since related how relieved he was to have someone sit next to him. He has since "adopted" this young lady and has realized God still has a job for him to do. What an example of an encourager that young person exhibited for all of the church family.

As a final thought, cards and emails are always welcome. I strongly encourage the church staff to appoint someone to send a card to the surviving spouse or caregiver once a month for the first year after the death of their loved one. It is especially important to continue to send a card or email once a year on the anniversary of their loved one's death. This lets the grieving family member know that someone still remembers. It is a small request, but it means so much to the survivor. Remember, cards and emails should not completely replace a personal visit.

Joy B. said that one of her most cherished memories after the sudden death of her husband was a basket of chocolates that lasted long after everyone was gone and the flowers had faded. She also has appreciated the email and Facebook messages she has received since—especially on the anniversary of his death and on special holidays. The most important message is this: Be a friend, and be present before, during, and after!

Near the beginning of this book, I mentioned the thought that we are taught to grow up, get a job, and have a family, but we are not taught how to grow old. In addition, we are not teaching our children how to relate to the elderly. Here are some suggestions how the church family can encourage young people and old people to interact and develop respect in both directions:

1. My father loved to receive mail. If a young person enjoys photography and has a printer, guide them to take a special photo and mail it to a homebound person. Using double-stick tape, they can adhere colored paper to the back (perhaps using a hole-punch or other decorative punch on the edges of the photo), write a quick "Thinking of You" and their name on the back, and mail a photo to a different elderly person each week.
2. Singing or talking with an elderly person goes a long way in making both the young person and the elderly feel important. Singing can be done in the home or any of the assisted living or nursing homes. Be sure to call ahead, and verify the time.
3. Encourage young people to listen. Guide them to ask for a story of the senior member's childhood and write it down or videotape it. Make a suggestion that they ask for war stories. Many times family members do not take the time to sit and listen to stories. What a treasure it would for family members to be able to have either a written or video record of their loved one's childhood!
4. Encourage mentoring. If the elderly are living at home, either a couple or a widow, see if one of them would allow the young people in to clean their house, wash windows, or cut the grass. Ask the elderly if they would allow this to be used as a means of teaching the young people how to do various jobs. Make it clear to the young person that this is a ministry. The young people may also like the elderly to teach them various skills such as auto care, gardening, painting, or perhaps a craft.

My basic thought and admonition is to be available and teach young people to love the elderly, not be afraid of them. We need to help the young realize they can learn from the older person. It is important that we train young people how to someday take care of their own elderly loved ones.

APPENDIX A

A-Z Scriptures for Meditation/Memorization

So many verses in the Bible are applicable to the caregiver. I have shared my own special list below:

A. A soft answer turneth away wrath: but grievous words stir up anger (Proverbs 15:1).

B. Be ye kind one to another, tenderhearted, forgiving one another, even as God for Christ's sake hath forgiven you (Ephesians 4:32).

C. Casting all your care upon him; for he careth for you (1 Peter 5:7).

D. Depart from evil, and do good; seek peace, and pursue it (Psalm 34:14).

E. Enter into his gates with thanksgiving, and into his courts with praise: be thankful unto him, and bless his name (Psalm 100:4).

F. Fear thou not; for I am with thee: be not dismayed; for I am thy God: I will strengthen thee; yea, I will help thee; yea, I will uphold thee with the right hand of my righteousness (Isaiah 41:10).

G. Go ye into all the world, and preach the gospel to every creature (Mark 16:15).

H. He maketh me to lie down in green pastures: he leadeth me beside the still waters (Psalm 23:2).

I. In my Father's house are many mansions: if it were not so, I would have told you. I go to prepare a place for you (John 14:2).

J. Jesus saith unto him, I am the way, the truth, and the life: no man cometh unto the Father, but by me (John 14:6).

K. Keep the door of my lips (Psalm 141:3).

L. Let your light so shine before men, that they may see your good works, and glorify your Father which is in heaven (Matthew 5:16).

M. My son, if sinners entice thee, consent thou not (Proverbs 1:10).

N. No man can serve two masters: for either he will hate the one, and love the other; or else he will hold to the one, and despise the other. Ye cannot serve God and mammon (Matthew 6:24).

O. give thanks unto the LORD; for he is good; for his mercy endureth for ever (1 Chronicles 16:34).

P. Put on the whole armour of God, that ye may be able to stand against the wiles of the devil (Ephesians 6:11).

Q. Quench not the Spirit (1 Thessalonians 5:19).

R. Restore unto me the joy of thy salvation and uphold me with thy free spirit (Psalm 51:12).

S. Suffer little children, and forbid them not, to come unto me: for of such is the kingdom of heaven (Matthew 19:14).

T. Trust in the LORD with all thine heart; and lean not unto thine own understanding (Proverbs 3:5).

U. Unto you is born this day in the city of David a Saviour, which is Christ the Lord (Luke 2:11a).

V. Verily I say unto you, Except ye be converted, and become as little children, ye shall not enter into the kingdom of heaven (Matthew 18:3).

W. What time I am afraid, I will trust in thee (Psalm 56:3).

X. eXcept a man be born again, he cannot see the kingdom of God (John 3:3).

Y. Ye must be born again (John 3:7).

Z. Zealous of good works (Titus 2:14).

APPENDIX B

Medical Terminology

I. Cardiopulmonary Resuscitation (CPR)

CPR is a procedure used when a patient's heart stops beating. It can involve compressions of the chest or electrical stimulation as well as respiratory assistance.

II. Do Not Resuscitate (DNR)(No-Code)

DNR is a physician's order not to attempt CPR if a patient's heart or breathing stops. The order is written at the request of the patient or family, but it must be signed by a physician to be valid. There are separate DNR versions for the home and the hospital.

III. Durable Power of Attorney for Healthcare (POA)

A document that designates the person we trust to make medical decisions on our behalf if we are unable

IV. Hydration

The process of providing water or fluid by mouth, tube, or intravenously

V. Intubation

The process of inserting a tube into a patient's trachea (windpipe) to help with breathing

VI. Life-Prolonging Treatment

Medical treatments that aim to cure or remedy an illness

VII. Living Will

A document stating a patient's wishes regarding medical treatments

VIII. Long-Term Care

Care that supports patients with chronic impairment for an indefinite period of time. It can be provided in nursing facilities, at home, or in the community.

IX. Percutaneous Endoscopic Gastrostomy (PEG)

A surgical procedure for inserting a tube through the abdominal wall and into the stomach to provide nutrition and hydration

X. Ventilator

A machine that forces air into a patient's lungs when he or she is unable to breathe independently

XI. Palliative Care (pronounced pal'-lee-uh-tiv)

a. A medical specialty focused on relief of the pain, stress and other debilitating symptoms of serious illness

b. Palliative care is not dependent on prognosis and can be delivered at the same time as treatment that is meant to cure us.

c. The goal is to relieve suffering and provide the best possible quality of life for patients and their families.

d. Palliative care relieves symptoms such as pain, shortness of breath, fatigue, constipation, nausea, loss of appetite, and difficulty sleeping.

e. It helps patients gain the strength to carry on with daily life.

f. It improves their ability to tolerate medical treatments, and helps them better understand their choices for care.

g. Overall, palliative care offers patients the best possible quality of life during their illness.

XII. Hospice

Considered a model of quality care, hospice focuses on relieving symptoms and supporting patients with a life expectancy of months, not years. Hospice involves a team-oriented approach to expert medical care, pain management, and emotional and spiritual support. The emphasis is on caring, not curing. In most cases, hospice care is provided to a patient in his or her own home. It also can be provided in freestanding hospice facilities, hospitals, nursing homes, and other long-term care facilities. Hospice care is offered for up to six months, renewable as necessary.

XIII. Common Treatment Options

a. Fluids

b. Antibiotics

c. Oxygen

d. Catheter

XIV. Optional Treatment Options

a. Feeding Tube/Peg Tube

b. Trach/Ventilator

c. CPR

APPENDIX C

List of Important Documents

Every adult should keep the following documents on file and designate at least one person who will know where to find the information (not so much what is on the list but where to find the list).

I. Power of attorney (POA)

II. Healthcare POA

III. Will

IV. Living will

V. Military service records

VI. Military discharge papers

VII. Family information
  - a. Date of birth
  - b. Full legal names
  - c. Location of birth certificates
  - d. Marriage license
  - e. Death certificate of spouse and/or divorce records

VIII. Insurance agent
  - a. Primary insurance
  - b. Secondary insurance

c. Medicare card

d. Long-term care policy

e. Life insurance

f. Disability

g. Veteran's benefits

h. Home insurance

i. Auto insurance

IX. Banking Information

a. Checking

b. Savings

c. Safety deposit box (including key location and name on box)

d. Ready cash

X. Investments (including financial advisor's name and phone number)

XI. Pension plan

XII. Property titles

a. Home

b. Auto

c. Land

d. Boat

e. Vacation property

XIII. Credit cards (includes all authorized account holders)

XIV. Prepaid plans

a. Funeral
b. Burial plots

XV. Monthly bills/providers

a. Lights
b. Water
c. Gas
d. Garbage pickup
e. Mortgage
f. Auto loan
g. Home phone
h. Cell phone
i. Internet
j. TV (satellite or cable service)

XVI. Current service contracts

a. Termite protection
b. Alarm system
c. Cleaning service
d. Yard maintenance
e. Pool care

APPENDIX D

Favorite Caregiver Tips

1. One capful of mouth wash (cheap generic brand from dollar store) in bedside commode kills bacteria and smells great
2. Rubber mat under bedside commode to catch drips
3. Rubber dotted socks (for both winter and summer) rather than slippers
4. Warm clothes/towels in clothes dryer when bathing (do not put them in the microwave)
5. Have a seat in the shower (stool or combination bench for the tub)
6. Shower head that comes down closer to the patient
7. Difficulty swallowing
    a. Crush meds and put in chocolate pudding
    b. Baby rice cereal
    c. Stage 3 baby food (not the tastiest option)
    d. Puree table food
8. Use cups with lids and a straw (prevents spilling and frustration with weak, shaky hands)
9. Disposable underwear (please call them "underwear," not diapers)

10. For men: if they cannot get out of bed at night without help, consider an external catheter (remember to clean well by pouring mouthwash down the tubing as well)—a doctor's order is needed for the catheter

11. Bed pads under sheet to protect mattress
    a. Baby bed mattress pad/blankets are the perfect size and easily washed
    b. Assurance pads size 23x36 (available at www.amazon.com)

12. Equipment
    a. Hospital bed
    b. Bedside commode
    c. Wheelchair (electric and/or portable)
    d. Lift chair/recliner
    e. Cane/walker or walker with seat

13. Lamp with remote control
    a. Plug lamp into a Christmas tree remote controller or the remote controller for indoor/outdoor lights available especially at Christmas
    b. Tie the remote within easy arm's reach

14. Always cold?
    a. Lap robes (thighs are usually the coldest)
    b. Twin size electric blanket in the winter (especially when sitting during the day and on the bed at night)
    c. Twin electric mattress pad (my dad loved this and they are also washable)

15. Photo screen with rotating pictures (these are somewhat small so hook it up to a TV or larger computer screen)
16. Cowbell to get our attention if we are in another part of the house
    a. Lifeline from the local healthcare facility or home health
    b. A baby monitor is also an option
17. Books on tape, e-readers, a lightweight computer or iPad, real books
    a. The font on the e-reader and the iPad can be enlarged to make it easier to read
    b. The local library is a great source for books on tape and real books
18. Calendar clearly marked with family birthdays, appointments, and holidays
19. Notepad and fat pen (for ease of use)
20. Sugar-free cough drops or candy unwrapped in a covered dish (helps with dry mouth)
21. Clock with large numbers (in direct line of eyesight)
22. White board hanging on the wall (in direct line of eyesight)
    a. Write words of encouragement
    b. Write daily reminders
    c. Tape cards/pictures received in the mail to the board

APPENDIX E

Additional Resources

- DVD/WORKBOOK – available on Amazon.com

  Miller, Valeri. *Changing MY Heart, GOD'S Path for the Caregiver*

  I have a companion DVD and workbook recommended for small groups or personal use. There are eight lessons, each thirty- to forty-five minutes in length.

- WEBSITE: www.biblicalcaregiving.com

  I publish a monthly newsletter with practical tips and spiritual encouragement.

- FACEBOOK: Biblicalcaregiving.com

- EMAIL: johnandvaleri@bellsouth.net

  I would love to hear from you!

Bibliography

1. C. P. Hia. "Commanded To Love", *Our Daily Bread*, Grand Rapids, MI September 9, 2010.

2. Beach, Shelly. *Ambushed by Grace* (page 37) Discovery House Publishers 2008

3. Cohen, Tom, CNN. Mickey Rooney tells Senate panel he was a victim of elder abuse. March 2, 2011

4. Sollitto, Marlo. Excerpt contributed by AgingCare.com, from the article "Loss of Taste in the Elderly".

CPSIA information can be obtained at www.ICGtesting.com
Printed in the USA
LVOW121147160513

334140LV00001B/3/P